Advisory Board

ASHE Higher Education Report: Volume 32, Number 1
Kelly Ward, Lisa E. Wolf-Wendel, Series Editors

Cost-Efficiencies in Online Learning

Katrina A. Meyer

Cost-Efficiencies in Online Learning
Katrina A. Meyer
ASHE Higher Education Report: Volume 32, Number 1
Kelly Ward, Lisa Wolf-Wendel, Series Editors

ISSN 1551-6970   electronic ISSN 1554-6306   ISBN 0-7879-8855-3

The ASHE Higher Education Report is part of the Jossey-Bass Higher and Adult Education Series and is published six times a year by Wiley Subscription Services, Inc., A Wiley Company, at Jossey-Bass, 989 Market Street, San Francisco, California 94103-1741.

For subscription information, see the Back Issue/Subscription Order Form in the back of this volume.

CALL FOR PROPOSALS: Prospective authors are strongly encouraged to contact Kelly Ward (kaward@wsu.edu) or Lisa Wolf-Wendel (lwolf@ku.edu). See "About the ASHE Higher Education Report Series" in the back of this volume.

Visit the Jossey-Bass Web site at **www.josseybass.com.**

Printed in the United States of America on acid-free recycled paper.

Contents

Executive Summary

What do we know about achieving cost-efficiencies through online learning? Perhaps more than many in higher education suspect, although plenty of questions remain to be answered. This report summarizes and analyzes the research literature that addresses cost-efficiencies of online learning, using a framework developed by Meyer (2005) and explained in the first chapter. The framework helps us disentangle influences on cost-efficiencies across various research studies to help extract trends and postulate conclusions. This report is a companion to an earlier ASHE-ERIC Higher Education Report, *Quality in Distance Education: Focus on On-Line Learning* (Meyer, 2002b), which discusses the research on how, when, and where online learning can work well for students and enhance quality. This report completes the picture by addressing cost issues, with a specific focus on cost-efficiencies.

The Framework

The framework comprises three elements based on the work of Rumble (2001). It includes two stages—development and delivery—and one overarching category—administration. To help break these large categories down further, seven factors are discussed: students, faculty, other staff, instructional design, content, infrastructure, and policy. By placing insights from the research studies where an element and a factor intersect (for example, where research on students enlightens costs related to delivery), we can group conclusions to determine their consistency and to uncover any interactions among or between cells. Such a review of research also begins to clearly identify what we know and the cells where little research exists.

Necessary Definitions

This work stresses research on cost-efficiencies or the relationship between inputs and outputs, with a primary focus on costs (see Rumble, 1997, 2001). Wherever possible, research on cost-effectiveness is reported, which captures the relationship of inputs to outputs and the focus on the value or quality of the outputs. But even though the focus is on cost, one should not assume that quality is sacrificed. In fact, this work requires that one suspend assumptions about the necessary relationship that quality requires greater expenditure of resources and that efficiency necessarily results in less effectiveness or lower quality. This work also requires an appreciation for costing methodologies and such terms as *fixed and variable costs, breakeven points,* and *budgeting;* these terms are essential for discussing when and where online learning can achieve the cost-efficiencies claimed for it by advocates.

Conclusions

Studies on online learning continue to be performed, and they will continue to push the boundaries of our knowledge of what can be cost-efficient. Thus, it is important to consider the following conclusions as tentative, soon to be replaced by better studies and deeper understanding of the issues. It is important for readers to take these conclusions as provisional, use and test them, and be prepared to modify them on the basis of further research. Moreover, students, market dynamics, and technologies will likely change. But in the meantime, these insights appear to be solidly founded on the research we have so far.

Development is more expensive than delivery. When critics charge that online learning is more expensive, they are more accurately describing the extra cost involved in developing courses and programs. To achieve cost-efficiencies, the higher cost of development must be worth it, both in terms of efficiency and student learning.

Development is where cost-efficiencies are made possible. So if development is costly, why do it? Because it is where the seed of cost-efficiency is planned for, planted, and made a reality. It is where Web designers and instructional designers combine with faculty to create a better learning experience for students and where the course design incorporates the substitution of capital for labor, lower-cost labor for higher-cost labor, and capital for capital. In each instance, the use of faculty is modified, and replaced by online modules, learning objects, virtual labs, online quizzes, automatic grading, and graduate assistants, peer tutors, or technical assistants who can answer students' questions. These changes allow institutions to use fewer capital resources and less faculty time. Faculty effort is reserved for developing courses, teaching higher-level skills, and other more important duties.

Delivery is where cost-efficiencies occur. Once designed, an online course can be delivered at lower cost than the traditional model by using less faculty time and more lower-cost labor. It can be delivered multiple times or in multiple sections at less instructional cost. And if offered to large numbers of students, the cost of development can be divided by larger numbers of students.

Administration costs but can also be cost-efficient. Many higher education institutions are investing in the online administrative services that modern students seem to prefer and states insist on: enterprise resource planning systems, online bill payment, online applications and registration, online courses, online library databases, and data collection and analysis to keep the institution informed of how things are operating. These costs are ongoing and support several functions of the college or university, not just online learning. But once installed and working, these services save time for students, faculty, and institutions.

Students create economies of scale—and some challenges, too. By their very numbers, students create economies of scale: the opportunity to divide the higher cost of development over more students, an argument for using the three substitutions in high-enrollment courses. It also means, however, that even smaller courses can achieve economics of scale if they are repeated often enough without substantially upgrading the course. But students bring other characteristics that affect efficiency: their willingness to learn more independently, their ability to equip themselves for online learning, their ability to pay greater fees, and so on.

Faculty time is precious. The focus of instructional redesign is to use faculty time differently—to use it less on activities that technology can do and more where the expertise of faculty matters most. This transformation of the faculty role is essential for achieving cost-efficiencies as well as improving quality for both faculty and students (Massy, 2002).

Other staff are key for instructional design to create cost-efficiencies. To redesign courses well and efficiently, higher education needs new staff with new skills: Web designers, instructional designers, and online course designers. And these individuals need to redesign courses that make the three substitutions in ways that improve learning and student retention. Not all design needs to be done by designers, however; some evidence exists that faculty, taught some of these skills, can make similar improvements in their online courses without using multiple staff or long development schedules. So at least some of the new staff should be expert in professional development for faculty.

The role of prepackaged content is unknown. The impact of preexisting online courses, learning objects, and freely available curricula on cost-efficiency has yet to be proved. This area is ripe for careful research studies that recognize the time spent on making these prepackaged elements workable for the course under design.

Infrastructure is a barrier, but it is essential. Despite a lack of definitive research on the role of a technical infrastructure on cost-efficiency, it makes sense that an institution with an insufficient infrastructure faces a different cost situation from an institution whose challenges are to keep abreast with demands on the network. One cannot conceive of proceeding with online learning without sufficient infrastructure. Outsourcing or leasing is an option, particularly for smaller institutions (Leach and Smallen, 2000).

The role of policies is unknown. This factor has been researched the least, but it is the area where the greatest need exists for sound answers. How do policies on setting tuition or the price of online courses affect cost-efficiencies? Will a policy encouraging the sharing of content work? How do policies on faculty workload, pay, promotion, tenure, or intellectual property affect cost-efficiencies or the faculty's willingness to engage in innovation? Does evidence exist that unbundling the faculty role will make it cost-efficient? Will policies that encourage students to use institutional resources efficiently work? Will having a strategic plan or vision improve the likelihood that cost-efficiencies will result? Will online learning achieve cost-efficiencies only if policies on seat time, class scheduling, class size, and the academic calendar fall by the wayside? What policies act as a brake on achieving cost-efficiencies, and what policies reward improving cost-efficiency?

Indications of change. It is possible that the studies reviewed as part of this work have a larger message for higher education: traditional assumptions about the relationship of cost to quality and assumptions about class size, faculty roles, and a dependence on lectures, classroom-based discussions, and face-to-face interactions are up for reassessment. If it is true that these assumptions are eroding—even if only a little and only among a few individuals in higher education—they represent a potentially enormous change in attitude and approach. They indicate a willingness to innovate and experiment and not be bound by the traditions and assumptions about learning and how it happens.

The message for states and institutions. It is clear that online learning can be cost-efficient. But—it takes resources, new staff, administrative services, and infrastructure. It requires that the goal of cost-efficiency be set up front rather than applied as an afterthought. It depends on thoughtful and careful design and a willingness to cost and budget carefully, test and assess, and modify based on early results. It is not for the faint hearted or weak willed. It does not happen overnight or on a whim. It is hard work. It entails higher costs to get to lower costs. It represents an enormous learning curve—for faculty and students, designers and other staff, and especially institutional and state leaders. Most important, it takes time.

More research is needed. Even more important, it takes a lot of people in a lot of institutions studying what they are doing, trying new tactics, assessing their effectiveness and efficiency, and sharing the results with others so they can build on what others have done. This enterprise depends on the willingness of institutions to try new things, possibly fail, and figure out why. It depends on the creativity and innovative spirit of individuals at institutions who must be willing to put a cost on their efforts. It depends on putting costs in perspective and ensuring that student learning is a final and best arbiter of whether an innovation is successful.

This process takes time and resources, intelligent and willing people, and an ability to look hard at our processes and policies. The good news is that achieving cost-efficiencies through online learning is possible, and we know some of the ways to achieve those cost-efficiencies right now.

Foreword

A cursory glance at any national newspaper, television network, or billboard advertising reveals that online learning is on the rise at all types of colleges and universities. Campuses widely advertise the opportunity for students to participate in higher education through online programs while being able to maintain connections with family and current jobs, and without having to move. Online delivery of courses expands the reach of higher education. In an increasingly competitive arena for students, online programs can tap into extended markets to attract additional students and expand programmatic offerings—an attractive proposition for campuses looking to increase enrollment and extend themselves beyond the traditional campus setting.

No longer the purview of a limited number of peripheral institutions, distance education today is in the mainstream of higher education. Yet, analysis and synthesis of research related to online learning has been limited leaving many to wonder about the costs and benefits of online learning and distance education. In a 2002 ASHE Report, *Quality in Distance Education: Focus on On-Line Learning,* Katrina Meyer helped address questions about the academic efficacy of online learning. Meyer told us to look more critically and thoroughly at research related to the how, when, and where of online learning in the interest of enhancing quality. Meyer helped fill a gap in understanding about quality, and in this current monograph—a companion to the 2002 volume—she addresses questions related to cost efficiencies, an important consideration in budget-conscious times.

On the surface it is easy to see online learning as a quick fix—a way to fairly rapidly increase access to a large number of geographically dispersed students. And, in fact, online programs have granted access to thousands of students who would have otherwise been limited in their ability to participate in higher education. But we know little about the financial costs of such expansion. In this monograph Meyer addresses questions such as: Is it economical for campuses to expand into online markets? What impact do such offerings have on traditional academic programs? What costs are involved for faculty? Do distance education program save campuses time and money? This monograph tackles these questions and others, and in doing so, provides campus faculty, administrators, and staff with invaluable information as they consider and reflect upon the expansion and reformulation of academic offerings using online delivery methods.

This monograph pushes readers to think differently about cost, quality, and efficiency not only in online contexts but in traditional contexts as well. The infusion of technology into the teaching process calls for everyone in higher education to think differently about traditional assumptions related to class size, faculty roles and rewards, class formats, and, above all, student learning and how it takes place in different contexts. Looking more closely at cost efficiencies in online contexts can help institutions think differently about cost efficiencies in other areas of their campus as well.

Kelly Ward
Series Editor

Published online in Wiley InterScience
(www.interscience.wiley.com) • DOI: 10.1002/aehe.3201

The Road Map to Cost-Efficiencies of Online Learning

THIS CHAPTER PROVIDES A ROAD MAP for understanding the review of studies on cost-efficiencies of online learning, including understanding why cost-efficiencies are so important to many higher education institutions and the framework used to categorize and discuss these studies. It discusses important definitions as well as the tools the reader will need for this trip, the assumptions that will need to be made (or unmade), and who the audience for such a trip ought to be. It should be an interesting trip, with some tollways, side trips, and occasional detours.

Why Be Interested in Cost-Efficiencies?

Why is there such interest in discovering cost-efficiencies in higher education, particularly through the application of online learning? Certainly most states have been experiencing hard financial times, largely the result of slumping economies; the loss of jobs and businesses in the airline, manufacturing, and service sectors, stagnant wage growth; and the growing demands for funding K–12 schools and health care. These pressures were exacerbated by the financial problems following the events of September 11, 2001, as well as earlier taxpayer revolts in the 1970s and 1980s that limited the taxing or spending authority of states. In 2003, twenty-three state legislatures were forced to cut higher education budgets (Arnone, 2004a), and at one time the combined deficits of the fifty state governments totaled $85 billion, the "highest number since the Great Depression" (White, 2003, p. 54). Even as it appears some state revenues may be improving, it is unclear whether those funds will go to higher education or other demands on state budgets such as K–12 education, Medicare, and transportation or returned to taxpayers in the form of tax cuts or refunds.

This bleak financial picture is made worse by a growing demand for higher education. Estimates by the National Center for Education Statistics (2002b) put the growth in college enrollments from 1990 to 2000 at 10.8 percent; enrollment growth from 2000 to 2012 could top 15 to 19 percent, with several states experiencing much higher growth rates. This demand for higher education comes from a growing number of high school graduates as well as adults who need to update or upgrade their skills. Estimating the number of adults returning to higher education is more difficult. Early estimates of potential students for online learning were based on the federal government's projection that one in seven adult workers would require professional development each year, translating into thirty million students in the United States or 128 million full-time equivalent (FTE) students worldwide (Duderstadt, 1999). The Conference Board of Canada (1991) estimates that "knowledge workers require at least the equivalent of three months of education or training every five years just to stay competent in their field" (Bates, 2000a, p. 5), resulting in thousands of new students for Canadian universities. In either estimate, the total projection seems almost impossible, both to realize and to satisfy. And there may be good reasons both estimates are optimistic (Meyer, 2003), as the estimation method relies on the assumption that government assessments of a need for training will translate into student enrollments and into online programs specifically.

These pressures of constrained resources and more students seem only to accentuate higher education's productivity problem, or as Heterick (1995) put it, academic productivity is "our pale horse" (p. 1), a reference to the Four Horsemen of the Apocalypse. Green (2000) calls academic productivity an oxymoron, a joke that is in turn funny and not so funny. The National Commission on the Cost of Higher Education (1998) takes a more serious stance, quoting data on the 57 percent increase in instructional cost from 1987 to 1996 and the 132 percent increase in average tuition for the same period at public four-year colleges and universities. Median family income rose 37 percent, disposable per capita income 52 percent, while the price of attending college (minus grants) rose 114 percent at public four-year institutions.

And although faculty share in the blame for this situation, so does technology, which adds to cost as it adds a "promise for making educational operations more efficient and less costly" (p. 17). The national commission (1998) called for "significant gains in productivity and efficiency. . . . through the basic way institutions deliver most instruction" by focusing on "alternative approaches to collegiate instruction" (p. 24) and student learning rather than time spent in the classroom. It also stressed the use of "efficiency self-reviews" (p. 23) and the use of accreditation to improve productivity, efficiency, and cost constraint (p. 31).

Tied to long-standing rules governing student-faculty ratios, faculty workloads, and class size, higher education's academic productivity has risen only with the addition of more faculty, which requires more resources. The introduction of technology exacerbated the problem with the "IT productivity paradox" (Finkelstein and Scholz, 2000, p. 5). In other words, despite large investments in technology, productivity is not improved and may be worsened (Fahy, 1998). This was a phenomenon in business as well, until various business processes and practices were rethought and revised, or as Friedman (2005) puts it, "The big spurts in productivity come when a new technology is combined with new *ways* of doing business" (p. 177, italics in the original). The productivity paradox—and identifying the new ways of doing the business of higher education—will be important issues for higher education's future and are an overall theme in this report.

In other words, productivity in higher education has traditionally been tied to receipt of more resources: more funding translated into more enrollments. This is not likely to be the case in the future. In the past several years, states have told some institutions to enroll more students at no, minimal, or some marginal funding from state coffers. This solution may be a necessary attempt by the state to generate greater productivity rather than an attempt by the institution to improve its productivity based on a better understanding or fundamental change of internal processes. Unfortunately, change forced from without rarely leads to insight, especially if institutional leaders retain hope that another budget year will turn the tide and result in more resources.

This is why Breneman's insight (2002) into the structural nature of states' problems with sustaining or growing resources is particularly useful. Hard times are here to stay, because current financial problems are the result of a number of forces that show little sign of abating. They include the demand for more funding for K–12 education as a result of student enrollment growth and No Child Left Behind; more funding needed for Medicare, welfare, prisons, and transportation; and the limits of taxpayers' willingness to continue to bear increased taxes. Further, state tax structures also create a portion of the problem, as some states depend inordinately on property taxes or sales taxes, which tend to be regressive and generate angst among taxpayers. It does not mean there is a perfect tax structure somewhere, as no one likes paying taxes, but the kind of tax and the rate at which it is imposed do affect taxpayers' support as well as the amount of funds available to states for funding services, including higher education.

Complicating these pressures is the tendency of states and institutions to off-load additional costs to students through new fees, higher tuition, or requirements for computers, Internet access, or particular software packages. These practices add to the cost of education for students and make it harder for states to increase access, especially access for low-income students.

In contrast to these trends are the mega-universities that Daniel (1996) focused on. Such mega-universities are institutions that enroll 117,000 (Payame Noor University in Iran) to 578,000 (Anadolu University in Turkey) students. Just at the time that universities in the United States were being criticized for their high costs and demands for funding, Daniel points out that the average cost per student in the United States was $12,500 and in the United Kingdom was around $10,000 but that the 11 mega-universities enrolled 2.8 million students at around $350 per student (Daniel, 1997). Were the lower costs per student achieved solely through the enormous enrollments or economies of scale? Was quality a problem? Not for the Open University, which enrolled 157,000 students in 1995 and is also known for its high-quality materials and use of lower-cost tutors. In any case, the experience of the mega-universities generated serious questions about how universities in the United States operate.

Online learning is introduced into this pressure-packed situation with both potential and promise to solve higher education's productivity problem at the same time it adds to the need for greater expenditures that in turn fuel greater pressure on institutional and state budgets. Is online learning, in this sense, a rescuer or a wolf in sheep's clothing? The question does not have a simple answer.

Online learning generated a long list of promises: it would help stem the growth in higher education budgets, avoid additional costs, increase access, reduce costs, improve cost-efficiencies, and offer mass customization (Bates, 2000b; Finkelstein and Scholz, 2000; Massy, 2003; Massy and Zemsky, 1995). It was the darling of legislators and governors, politicians and businesspersons. And it caught on: more than 90 percent of public institutions provide some sort of distance learning and enroll 3,077,000 students in all varieties of distance offerings (National Center for Education Statistics, 2003). Enrollments in completely online *programs* totaled 937,000 students in 2004 (Carnevale, 2005), a figure that is expected to grow to 1.2 million students in 2005, or 7 percent of the total student enrollment in degree-granting institutions. Enrollments in online *courses* in fall 2003 totaled 1.9 million students, having grown 20 percent from fall 2002 (Allen and Seaman, 2004). No estimate yet exists of how many courses use elements of online learning to improve student learning or enhance the quality of on-campus classes, but the figure probably runs into the millions.

One promise, to improve the quality of student learning, has been researched. An earlier ASHE-ERIC Higher Education Report, *Quality in Distance Education: Focus on On-Line Learning* (Meyer, 2002b), provides a review of the research literature on how and when it can improve student learning. Swan (2003) and DuMont (2002) have produced similar reviews of research on questions of quality. "Quality" is not just the result of high-quality materials or having good professors, but it documents student learning through various assessment methods. In any case, one can be relatively confident that student learning can be achieved through online learning, if it is well designed. Many of the studies that follow document how student learning improves even as cost-efficiencies are gained. You can have both quality and cost savings if you follow design principles that have been proven to produce both.

Pressure built on institutions, however, to use online learning to improve productivity and to break the traditional assumptions about how productive higher education could be. As a result, a growing number of efforts were undertaken to cost online learning fairly and to experiment with different ways to improve the efficiency of the higher education enterprise. Some were home-grown studies, an attempt to answer questions about how to improve productivity at one institution; still others resulted as a coordinated attempt to explore practices together and to standardize measurements and budgeting so that studies at a few institutions could be compared. As the number of studies grew, it was necessary to capture what could be learned in a way that drew across studies, pulling out ideas and practices that occurred in several studies and capturing the principles in a way others could understand. The framework below is an attempt to categorize and specify lessons learned across these studies.

The Framework for Unraveling Research on Cost-Efficiencies

A growing number of careful research studies is helping to unravel where, when, and how online learning can be cost-efficient. A conceptual framework proposed by Meyer (2005) can help us to get our arms around the complexities of online learning, to break that complexity into conceptual areas, and to understand how changes in one area can interact with other areas and impact the cost-efficiency of courses or programs. This framework is based on the work of several researchers. Rumble (2001) first separated cost analyses into two stages (development and delivery) and a category (administration) that included both stages. Many things happen in these stages and within administration, and several subcategories therefore were needed to disentangle issues or areas that could affect cost-efficiency in Rumble's groups. After a review of the literature of many studies, seven subcategories were defined: students, faculty, other staff, course design, content, infrastructure, and policy. To talk about these groups and categories, however, a simpler language and visual framework were needed.

Development, delivery, and administration are termed "elements" in this framework, a reference to their basic or essential part in online education. The various subcategories referred to above are called "factors" for their role in making online learning what it is (both definitions are from *Webster's New World*

EXHIBIT 1
Proposed Framework of Elements and Factors

Factors / Elements	Development	Delivery	Administration
Students			
Faculty			
Other Staff			
Course Design			
Content			
Infrastructure			
Policy			

SOURCE: Meyer, 2005, p. 20.

College Dictionary, 1999). These terms have been chosen to help designate potential roles for these constituent parts of online learning and to make the discussion clearer and more precise. Exhibit 1 is a visual representation of the elements and factors and the "cells" where interactions might be found.

This report discusses the research that has been conducted to clarify components in the different cells of the framework. It also draws attention to ways in which factors interact or where decisions in one area interact with characteristics in another area or where two good decisions may well produce a counterproductive result. Where feasible, cells or questions that have not been studied will also be highlighted. This review answers one major broad question: How can institutions of higher education improve the cost-efficiency of online learning?

Tools for the Journey

Before beginning this journey through the research that will help fill in some of the framework, we need some definitions and tools to help make the journey clearer. First, let us clarify what is meant by "cost-efficiency." Efficiency indicates a relationship between inputs and outputs, and "cost-efficiency" clarifies that the relationship is focused primarily on costs; Rumble (1997) and others use the term in this way. Outputs are variously defined in the studies reviewed, but most include student enrollments or completions, credit hours, or graduations. In other words, if outputs can be increased with a less than proportional increase in inputs, it is more cost-efficient (Ash, 2000). A variation on this concept is a more absolute definition of "efficient," which implies that an optimum has been found between minimizing costs and maximizing effects (Moonen, 1997), but this definition has not been used in the studies reported herein.

"Cost-effectiveness" looks at the relationship between inputs and outputs, but in this case the outputs are characterized by their value or quality (see Levin and McEwan, 2001, for a guide to conducting cost-effectiveness analyses). For example, an online program might produce twenty graduates, but ten cannot pass their board exams; the program may be cost-efficient, but it is not cost-effective. Several studies have been included that address cost-effectiveness, but the majority of studies do not attempt this analysis, so this report and its title use the term *cost-efficiencies.*

"Cost-benefit" analysis is a more specific type of analysis that requires both costs and benefits to be measured in monetary terms (see Cukier, 1997, for several examples). It is not likely, however, that this analysis will be applied to the outputs of higher education institutions in the near future (Moonen, 1997), and presumably it is not likely to be applied to online learning soon.

"Productivity" is the ratio of outputs to inputs or, more generally, the ratio of benefits to costs. So the term can be used as an analogue of both cost-efficient and cost-effective, which might be confusing. Economics tends to define these terms in very specific equations, so if the reader is interested in economic precision, you may need to refer to an economics textbook. It is fair to say, however, that the layman tends to use the word *productivity* to emphasize the amount of what is produced. "Cost-efficient" tends to focus attention on costs and efficiency in production.

Definitions of terms also vary in the studies reviewed as well as the definitions of categories of costs. This angle is important to unravel so that results can be categorized into the appropriate cell of the framework, but if you decide to read the original texts, pay careful attention to how that particular author has defined and calculated their costs. Studies might place paying copyright fees into development, delivery, or administration, depending on what makes sense to the institution.

It also is important to understand that different studies use different costing strategies. Although costing has been called "weighing air" (Ash and Bacsich, 1999, p. 2), "murky" (Hislop, 2001b, p. 201), "nebulous" (Milam, 2000), studying the "shape of jello" (Ehrmann, 2004), and "very complex" (Bishop and SchWeber, 2001, p. 178), some excellent work has been done recently on costing by various bodies interested in online learning and technology. The main costing strategies used in the studies reviewed are the Flashlight Cost Analysis Handbook (http://www.tltgroup.org/programs/fcai.html), the KPMG model (which is very close to the Flashlight model), the Activity-Based Costing (ABC) method (Bates, n.d.), the Technology Costing Methodology (TCM) (http://www.wcet.info/projects/tcm), the Cost of Supporting Technology Services (COSTS) (Leach and Smallen, 2000), and Morgan's online costing tool (2000) (http://www.marshall.edu/distance). Costing methods from the National Association of College and University Business Officers (NACUBO) (2002) and the Delaware Cost Studies (University of Delaware, 2002), which are used to calculate the cost of on-campus activities, have not been used in the studies reviewed for this report. These approaches cost "undergraduate instruction" (National Association of College and University Business Officers, 2002) or instructional costs by discipline or faculty type (University of Delaware, 2002) but do not provide data specifically on online coursework.

To understand costs of online coursework requires that the institution disaggregate costs in much greater detail or granularity. Activity-Based Costing has been a more popular method for costing online courses, because online courses have been a discrete but often modest activity in traditional institutions. Thus, costing online coursework is different from costing on-campus programs in terms of understanding how cost structures of online coursework are different from traditional courses and attempting to provide a more granular understanding of what is happening in an online course or how faculty time is spread across online courses and other important activities. ABC is therefore different from many other costing approaches, because it attempts to cost various activities (registering a student or preparing a PowerPoint presentation, for example) rather than by budgetary line item (faculty salaries, for example) or allocation of existing departmental or college-level budgets (Massy, 2003). Faculty salaries in this case are broken down into the various activities faculty do rather than being lumped together as a whole. Unfortunately, ABC has been criticized for depending on faculty's completing time sheets accurately and precisely when many faculty view such time sheets as administrative oversight that does not recognize how activities can serve multiple functions; they argue that their activities are too difficult to break down into minutes. Therefore, ABC may lack credibility among those who may expect precise and accurate information, but it is the only costing method that attempts to break apart different functions so that they can be useful in understanding separate activities. Perfect accuracy may be impossible but worth tolerating if the institution can better understand how and when different activities contribute to costs.

Models overlap, and ABC appears to be an element of Flashlight and TCM, perhaps because of its early development and popularization by Levin (1983) and Bates (n.d.). One likely misunderstanding is that costing is a way to identify and minimize costs; Peter Drucker (n.d.) indicates that activity-based accounting is particularly well suited for maximizing yields or creating value rather than minimizing waste or inefficiencies. It is important to realize that several reasons may motivate an institution to undertake a costing exercise: it wants to identify, understand, and control costs; it wants to identify costs so they can be included when setting prices, it wants to demonstrate increased cost-efficiency or to assess whether the cost of doing online learning is within its present or future means or capacity (Rumble, n.d., p. 5). These motivations matter, as they set the scene and purpose for costing. But costing methods differ: one method may choose to add overhead costs of one type to the cost of an online course, while another may choose to add a different set of overhead costs or none at all. Therefore, choosing which costing strategy to use is a professional and institutional decision based on needs, preferences, or contexts that make sense to the institution in that situation. Each costing method appears to have its advantages and disadvantages, costs left in or ignored as the case may be. TCM includes the costs borne by others such as students, while other costing methods do not. What is important is that the method is used consistently across all programs and informs institutional understandings and decisions. When comparing research studies, however, it is important to recognize that absolute results naturally vary, depending on the costing method chosen or institution-specific decisions made during the costing process. No benchmarks are available yet to compare online course or program costs, largely because of the variety of costing approaches used and the various ways institutions tailor their costing approaches to their own needs. But costs may also vary from institution to institution, even if they are using the same costing method, as a result of decisions made that are extraneous to the costing method. That is why the focus is less on the cost per student (unless there is a comparison embedded in the study and the costing was done exactly the same for different types of courses or programs) but more on what practices created greater cost-efficiency as they affect students, faculty, other staff, instructional design, content, infrastructure, or policy.

Last, professionals use a profusion of terms that are confusing to the neophyte: learning that is online, Web based, mediated, distributed, distance, technology mediated, telelearning, and e-learning. Each term has a particular meaning to the author or researchers, and some of them are preferred by professionals in one country but not another. This report uses "online learning," which includes various uses of the Internet and includes many other uses included in the terms above. But if the particular study being reviewed uses a different term—telelearning, for example—that is the term used in that discussion. It may well be that telelearning included more than just online learning, but the study had some important message for understanding cost-efficiencies. This approach may be a bit confusing, but until the field standardizes its terminology, we shall have to make certain accommodations to the proliferation and exuberance of our terms and shifting definitions.

Necessary Assumptions

This work is based on destroying assumptions, and the reader may need to assess his or her willingness to let go of some preconceptions. Some critics of online learning charge that achieving cost-efficiencies at the expense of quality or student learning is unthinkable, and most institutions would not willingly agree to do so. Plenty of evidence exists, however, that online learning can perform as well as traditional classroom teaching and can increase student learning for many students (Meyer, 2002b). So if an institution wishes to explore improving cost-efficiencies through the use of online learning, the literature and this report contain plenty of good evidence that student learning will be improved.

The second assumption up for questioning is the conventional wisdom (Massy, 2003, p. 246) that cost and quality are intricately and tightly tied together (see Figure 1). This assumption proposes that the only way to improve quality is to spend more and that, conversely, spending less means lower quality. The tight clustering of the points in Figure 1 implies that "faculty and administrators can do little to improve efficiency" (p. 245). The lower graph implies that spending must increase with enrollment if quality is to be held constant (p. 246). This illustration is an excellent example of "production functions" or assumptions about how teaching and learning must occur (such as rules about class size) that have dictated academic productivity and

FIGURE 1
Cost and Quality: The Conventional Wisdom

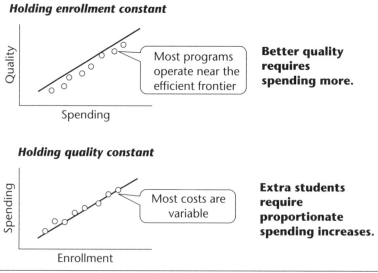

SOURCE: Massy, 2003, p. 246.

kept it from being improved. To continue to read this report requires that you be willing to put these assumptions aside.

The third assumption that must be questioned is the usual expectation that one publication can provide all the answers. Given the number of new technologies being developed, new teaching methods being used with those technologies, and new studies being undertaken each year, the answers sought may be a moving target. The reader is wise to be cautious and flexible and to stay open for new developments, as new techniques and practices may be developed that can improve efficiency and effectiveness of online learning in a marked way.

Who Should Be Interested?

Five audiences will likely be open to the findings of this report. First, higher education administrators from both the academic and financial sides of the institution may find it helpful to see how to achieve cost-efficiencies through online learning. Second, higher education system leaders and planners may find it useful to contemplate what it will take—in terms of funding, time, and effort—to achieve those cost-efficiencies and begin to improve the system's use of constrained resources. Third, this report may also be helpful to state and legislative leaders who need to understand the issues faced by higher education institutions attempting to use online learning to improve efficiency and increase access and who will, it is hoped, come to temper their optimism with a realistic and grounded enthusiasm for online learning. These leaders need to understand that technology is no magic bullet and that solutions are neither easy nor simple—and that one solution will not fit all instances. But there are answers to improve cost-efficiencies, although it will take time and effort and further experimentation to unravel them. Fourth, instructional designers and faculty developers may find some good ideas or approaches to improving what they do. Finally, faculty who are or want to teach online may find some of these insights helpful. Frankly, faculty could produce more cost-efficiencies across the full range of courses offered online in whole or in part if they are willing and able to apply some of the ideas that improve cost-efficiencies. In any case, readers should finish this report with a better understanding of what it will take to achieve cost-efficiencies through online learning and a growing willingness to do so.

The Road Ahead

The next chapter, "Research on the Elements of Online Learning," describes and integrates the research and literature on the elements, and "Research on the Factors of Online Learning" performs the same function for research on the factors. Wherever possible, interactions among the cells and holes, as well as cells where no research informs the analysis, are identified. "What Does It Mean for Institutions and States?" summarizes the major points of this review and discusses its implications for institutions and states, and the concluding chapter, "What Do We Know? What Research Is Needed?" returns to what we know and do not know about achieving cost-efficiencies, which dictates a research program to answer questions left unanswered by this review of the literature.

Research on the Elements of Online Learning

T HIS CHAPTER REVIEWS THE ELEMENTS of the framework presented in the previous chapter and introduces the reader to a number of useful concepts that can inform an understanding of relationships between the elements, especially the higher costs of development to the lower costs of delivery. Although it may feel like a digression, these terms and concepts are important to understanding when and where and whether online learning is appropriate for the institution and when and where and whether it can be used cost-efficiently. The chapter closes with several cautions that highlight a number of unresolved issues relating to costing online learning.

Terms to Aid Our Understanding

The higher cost of development for online courses and programs necessitates the use of two terms that are helpful in the following discussion. *Fixed costs* refers to costs paid no matter how many students are enrolled, and *variable costs* refers to costs that vary depending on the number of students in a class (Jones, 2001).

Fixed costs for online learning include the substantial costs of course and content development, including the time of faculty, instructional designers, technicians, and support staff. Added to these fixed costs are certain administrative costs, including a portion of the cost of Internet connections, servers/networks, computers, maintenance and support, and production studios. Because the online course or program is likely to be only one user of these services—which also support administrative and on-campus services—it

Cost-Efficiencies in Online Learning 15

FIGURE 2
Cost of Mediated/Online Instruction

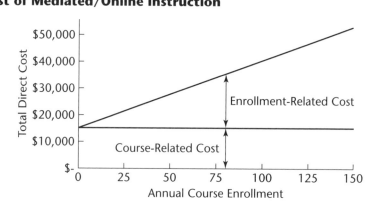

SOURCE: Jewett and Henderson, 2003, p. 18.

would not be reasonable for the online programs to bear the full cost of these now-essential services.

Variable costs include the instructor's (faculty, graduate assistants, or other teaching staff) time spent teaching or assessing student learning.

Because the fixed costs of an online course or program are the same whether the course enrolls one student or one thousand, it can be conceptualized as a base to which the variable cost—which depends on the number of students enrolled—is added. Figure 2 illustrates this relationship. Fixed costs make up the "course-related cost" of the baseline, and variable costs may be characterized by the "enrollment-related cost" of the sloped line.

This relationship can be contrasted with the usual cost relationship of traditional classroom instruction. In most cases, the cost of traditional instruction is the time spent by faculty to update their course or develop a new course, which does not require the time of anyone other than the faculty person involved. Doing so produces relatively low fixed costs. The cost of satisfying growing enrollments is basically the cost of opening a new section of the class with an instructor whose salary and classroom costs (if the classroom is rented) rise in a stepwise fashion (see Figure 3).

These figures do not represent an exact relationship but help us conceptualize the relationship of costs—and type of cost—to student enrollments. They help us understand that the cost of development is a fixed cost that must

FIGURE 3
Cost of Classroom Instruction

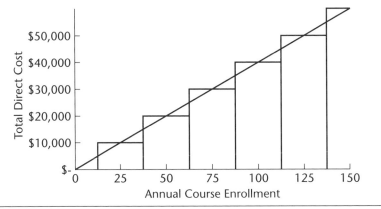

SOURCE: Jewett and Henderson, 2003, p. 17.

somehow be recouped, either by funding a portion of this cost by grants, allocating a portion of this cost to the price of the course, or estimating when the full cost of development is "covered" by having sufficient student enrollments through repeated offerings of the course.

The ratio of fixed to variable costs is an important calculation and helps us understand to what extent an institution has invested in higher development costs. The ratio of fixed to variable costs for the Open University is two thousand to one, while traditional U.K. universities run eight to one (Finkelstein and Scholz, 2000, p. 19).

Another calculation is also informative. At what point does online learning begin to cost less than traditional classes? This concept has several terms, including *crossover point,* the point on the line (see Figure 4) where revenue finally exceeds costs and the number of enrollments needed to do so. Another term, *breakeven point,* captures essentially the same idea. Unfortunately, the crossover point is different for every cost study, as it depends on what costs have been included (how much overhead must be covered), the cost of instructional staff (full-time faculty, for example, cost more than part-time instructors), and other assumptions. The label "clsrm inst" in Figure 4 is the cost of classroom instruction, and "clsrm + IT" is classroom instruction with added technology. (These lines capture the classic "bolt-on" or "add-on" conditions, where the cost of

Cost-Efficiencies in Online Learning

FIGURE 4
Total Direct Costs for Various Types of Instruction

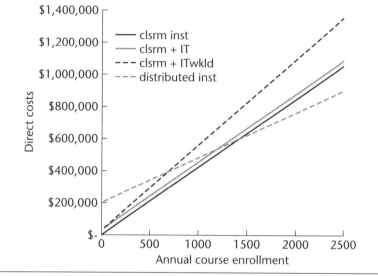

SOURCE: Jewett, 2000, p. 41.

technology is added to the regular cost of instruction; thus, this line is always higher than "clsrm inst.") The label "clsrm + ITwkld" assumes that instructors absorb the added workload on a volunteer basis, which has been commonplace but may be limited in the future; "distributed inst" is for a purely online or distributed education. The two important factors to notice in this figure are that the line for "distributed inst" begins at a higher cost level than the others because of its higher development costs but that at some point (fourteen hundred students in this graph) begins to cost less than the other modes of instruction. Again, the precise number of students when distributed or online education begins to pay off in lower costs will be different for other institutions, but the point should be calculated so that the institution can have this information as it makes decisions about allocation of resources or offering courses online.

Another example of the calculation of the crossover point is the study by Jewett and Henderson (2003), which looked at the cost of mediated courses at Washington State University using the TCM. Two different calculations for the cost of mediated courses yielded two different crossover points. When the calculation did not include the full cost of development (especially faculty time), the crossover point occurred at twenty students; when the calculation did include faculty time, the crossover point occurred at fifty-seven students (p. 25), illustrating the importance of decisions made during costing (more particularly, which costs to include and which costs to exclude).

One last term that might be useful is the concept of *unused* or *underused capacity.* The previous calculations cannot capture this concept, but it is essential to understanding why many leaders outside academe believe that higher education institutions can be more productive. It has not been defined or quantified or carefully studied, and it is not clear whether capacity can be perfectly or maximally used. In any case, it is a concept that needs to be incorporated in future institutional studies on cost-efficiencies of online learning.

The Elements: Development, Delivery, and Administration

Perhaps no author has done more to identify and discuss the implications of the cost of online learning than Rumble (1997, 2001). Rumble is professor of distance education management at Open University and has published extensively on issues of costs and costing for distance education. Rumble's early articles preceded those of many researchers included in this review, and it therefore may be fair to say that he was largely influential in defining our understanding of the types of costs involved in online learning, how they operate, and how or whether they can be controlled. Therefore, it makes sense to use his distinctions of "development," "delivery," and "administration" as stages and types of costs.

The separation of development and delivery into different categories has five advantages. First, it recognizes the higher costs of developing online courses and programs. Second, that cost of development can be treated much like a capital cost and annualized or spread out over the course of a year or more. Third, it allows institutions to uncover the lower cost of delivery if certain conditions are met. Fourth, it recognizes that the costs of administration are stage neutral; that is, they cannot be allocated to just development or just delivery but must be categorized as a need for the entire program. Fifth, the category "administration" recognizes that online learning consumes and contributes to an institution's overhead and should not have a "'free' ride" (2001, p. 78).

Rumble is concerned not only about understanding why online learning costs what it does in an individual course or program but also about the provision of tools for institutions to make better, more informed decisions about whether and how to pursue online learning. In other words, his detailed categories encourage institutions to raise their decision making to a conscious, data-driven process that ought to lead to fewer surprises in the long run. For those institutions that understand the costs and choose to pursue online initiatives, it is more likely the choice will be based on a more careful and thoughtful review of facts in the context of the institution's mission and vision.

The following review describes for each element first what Rumble included in the element and then reviews other research that has been conducted on costs included in that element. Where necessary, information that is not based on research is included if it has value for future researchers.

The Cost of Development: Higher for a Reason

Rumble (2001) includes eight categories of costs necessary to develop e-materials or online courses. Table 1, based on Appendix 1 in Rumble (2001), summarizes the contents of these categories.

This list of costs, although comprehensive, may not emphasize the nature of some costs or phrase the costs as others might. This difference does not invalidate Rumble's work but can make his work richer. For example, the concept of up-front learning in Arvan and others (1998) is more than just training on the use of new software; it also includes the acquisition of individual and organizational knowledge that is essential for doing online learning well and cost-efficiently. This concept seems more than what may be implied by training, but it can certainly be incorporated into that term. Trying to cost such learning seems impossible, however, given current cost accounting structures or the ability to put either a time or a moment on when an individual or an organization learns something. Although learning may happen in a moment, it sometimes takes a lot of preparation to achieve that momentary insight.

TABLE 1
Development Costs

Expenditure	Description
Materials	Includes course syllabus or outline, textbooks, texts with Web-based content, reference materials, images, audio, video, simulations, virtual reality
Staffing	Includes instructional design, content development, text authoring, software development, multimedia design and production, course-specific software development, content integration and testing, posttest modification, and training
Staff equipment	Computers and software, provided by the institution or staff
Staff expenses	Internet service provider
Copyright clearance	
Materials production	Text, audio, video, graphics, and software production, including staff time and supplies, to produce a CD-ROM, for example
Annual revision of materials	New assignments, examination questions
Developmental testing of course	Payments to course testers, general running costs of developmental testing

SOURCE: Rumble, 2001, pp. 89–90.

Another example of a possible addition to or clarification of this list is Morgan's inclusion of librarian support costs during development (2000), which may be implied by "staff" in Table 1, but it is fair to specify this cost to be clear.

Other additions involve the design and development of student assessments and course or program evaluations, which although not specifically labeled as such in the Rumble list, are important to U.S. universities. Designing assessment of student learning into every course and degree program, whether offered online or on campus, is an essential requirement for many accreditation processes. Morgan (2000) includes evaluation as a hidden cost, one that should be expressly included in the calculation of staff time and effort, and Ash (2000) makes a strong case for evaluation and understanding its costs. Lockee, Moore, and Burton (2002) stress the importance of designing appropriate evaluation strategies for distance education, focusing on student learning outcomes, student attitudes, other programmatic or institutional outcomes (such as increasing market reach, faculty promotions, adoption of innovations, and organizational changes), and implementation concerns of faculty, students, and the organization.

Additional costs such as library acquisitions, online library resources, and staff for information technology (IT) help desks certainly are related to development. But these types of services are difficult to apportion between development and delivery and are therefore put into "administration" in this framework. An institution may wish to try separating these costs into development or delivery, but it is likely that the decision may need a rubric or detailed accounting information to decide where to place the cost. For example, if a library acquisition is specifically and only for the online program, perhaps a percentage of the cost can be allocated to development and the remainder to delivery, but the percentage would need to be based on some rationale or figures of use available to the institution. On the other hand, it may make sense to simplify this entire process and place library support under administration.

Let us proceed with a review of the research on development costs with a focus on breaking down development costs into areas where decisions have cost implications and we have some data. First, it is important to remember that the media chosen directly affect the cost of the online course or program. It takes $2 to digitize a book chapter, $20 to $50 to have a work-study student or media specialist videotape a faculty lecture, $20 to $200 for an hour of faculty time, $200 to $2,000 for sixty minutes of unedited classroom video, $20,000 for thirty minutes of production-quality lecture, $100,000 for sixty minutes of commercial-quality video, and $100,000 to $400,000 for commercial-quality digital or computer simulation (Green, 1997, p. 4). Multimedia (such as animations and interactive programs) can double the production cost to $120,000 to $250,000 (Bodain and Robert, 2000). Print, audiocassettes, and prerecorded instructional television are lower in cost than developing CD-ROMs or video, but simulations and virtual reality are even more expensive because they require staff with specialized expertise or more time of all staff, including faculty, instructional designers, and technicians, to develop (Bates, 1995; Rumble, 2001). It makes sense that development costs would be lower for a hybrid course that uses some preprogrammed or multimedia materials than for a fully online or multimedia course.

For this reason, a study by Ellis and Cohen (2001) is interesting, because it attempted to assess students' perceived value of different materials, including higher-cost video, audio, and animation and lower-cost interaction and text. Students perceived the benefit of each mode to be nearly equal, ranging from 2.78 (the lowest rating) for video to 3.0 (the highest rating) for text. But the cost of each choice was not equal: video had a cost (scaled cost, not the actual figure) of 5.0, animation 3.75, audio 3.0, interaction 2.0, and text 1.25. Although the relationship to learning outcomes was not provided, it is clear that sometimes choosing to use media that entails a higher development cost may not be necessary—or even preferred by students. In other words, the cost-effectiveness of certain media is still an open question, although developers might for cost-efficiency reasons choose to use media that are lower in cost to develop until better data on cost-effectiveness of higher-cost media are available.

A related issue is the choice of developers to design lesser or greater interaction into the course, which in turn may require less or more faculty time during the delivery stage. Geith and Vignare (2001), in making this point, characterize a relationship between interaction and cost whereby courses that capture and distribute expert content in a "transmission" or "broadcast" mode are much less costly and demanding of faculty resources than courses that rely on student interaction with faculty and with other students, which faculty may still need to monitor, comment on, and evaluate. (Nevertheless, interaction is an important quality consideration, so its elimination based on a need to lower costs would be counter to improving student learning.)

A cost analysis by Geith and Cometa (1999) comparing distance education and on-campus courses at Rochester Institute of Technology confirms the relationship between development and delivery costs for the two types of instruction. When average costs by activity were calculated, the relationship of development to delivery costs was inversely related. The cost of development for the asynchronous courses was three times larger than for the on-campus courses, but the delivery costs (combining the categories of presentation and interaction) for the asynchronous courses were 12 percent less than the on-campus courses. This relationship (of higher development costs and lower operating or delivery costs) is confirmed in studies by Whalen and Wright (1999), Harley, Maher, Henke, and Lawrence (2003), Bartolic-Zlomislic and Bates (1999), Morgan (2000), and many others. Harley, Maher, Henke, and Lawrence (2003) studied a redesigned technology-enhanced Chemistry 1A course (a gateway course for many disciplines): three-quarters of the additional development cost was recovered through savings experienced in the delivery of the course in year 1; year 2 saw lower development costs and more than $100,000 in total savings. In another example, Morgan (2000) found that 48 percent of the costs of online courses at Marshall University were for development, 36 percent were for teaching (or delivery), and 16 percent were for technology and infrastructure (administration). In other words, the cost of development is consistently higher than the cost of delivery.

Capper and Fletcher (1996) and Jung and Rha (2000) in earlier reviews of the literature on cost-effectiveness of online learning found that online learning could indeed be cost-effective but that it depended on how frequently the course was revised, as each revision added to development costs, requiring additional course offerings to break even. They also found that the media chosen and type and amount of student support added to the cost of development.

The literature abounds with various estimates of the cost of developing an online course, from $2,660 to $21,170 (in Canadian dollars) per student-hour (Bates, 1995, p. 197) or from $6,000 to $1 million for a three-credit course (Arizona Learning Systems, 1998, pp. 13–14). "Simple outlines and assignments are the cheapest at $6,000, followed by text ($12,000), text with reference materials ($18,000), images ($37,500), audio and video ($120,000), simulations ($250,000), and virtual reality ($1 million)" (Rumble, n.d., p. 3). These estimates confirm an earlier point that various decisions about what media to use, what design is optimal, and what learning outcomes are intended combine to result in a very wide range of costs. To put it more simply, you can spend as much as you want, or you can spend less and still probably achieve similar outcomes.

The higher cost of development should not translate into an argument that a course or materials should not be well designed (Jones and Matthews, 2002). Irrespective of the media chosen, the course can incorporate principles of active learning or problem-based learning, which are known to be effective. But doing so requires the addition of expertise in instructional design, which most faculty may not have at the outset; faculty, however, may quickly acquire such expertise as they work with experts in pedagogy, instructional design, and course management systems. These new staff and the time it takes staff (including faculty) to develop new online courses and materials are the main reason that this type of instruction can be more expensive. (Research that specifically addresses faculty and other new staff is included in the next chapter.)

How else may development costs be recouped? Robinson (2001) has a useful approach that includes "re-purposing" materials so that there is greater opportunity to recoup development costs. Robinson calls this approach "transformative income generation" (p. 1), which simply involves developing a product and (1) repackaging it into different sizes, (2) disseminating it to different markets, or (3) remarketing it for a different constituency (p. 2). The example used is of an M.B.A. program that was repurposed into a certificate program and disseminated as continuing education for the working professional or adult education for seniors. Another example of repurposing is the promotion of learning objects—small, discrete learning units—that faculty can use in new course settings. Learning objects are discussed in greater detail in the next chapter in the section on content.

Several questions must beg answers. Can the cost of development decline? Can efficiencies occur during development? How can we learn to do it better and more efficiently? Now we turn our attention to the area of delivery costs, which bear the burden of making lower costs a reality.

The Cost of Delivery: The Potential for Lowering Costs

Rumble (2001) includes eight categories of delivery costs, as summarized and described in Table 2. Two items have been clarified on this chart. First, "instructor" is used rather than "tutor," because tutor tends to be defined

TABLE 2
Delivery Costs

Expenditure	Description
Materials delivery	Postage, courier, and so on resulting from the distribution of physical goods
Materials reception expenses	Expenses incurred by students, including the cost of receiving materials and printing them or purchasing materials
Student/instructor equipment	Network charges, computers, printers, and software for both students and instructors
Student/instructor expenses	Payments to Internet service provider or connection charges for time online; increased energy costs, insurance for equipment, and equipment repair
Cost of student time	Opportunity cost for students who could be doing paid work instead of classwork. Also applies to employers and the self-employed
Instructor time	Tuition varies whether full-time or part-time staff teach a course and how much time instruction requires from the instructor
Student/instructor helpdesk	Staffing a helpdesk for both students and instructors for help with routine technical questions
Call costs	Toll-free access to the helpdesk or other support functions

SOURCE: Rumble, 2001, pp. 91–92.

differently in the United States from the United Kingdom. Second, the original descriptor of the cost category of "instructor time" was "tuition," but "instructor time" captures the description used by Rumble and ensures that the issue remains instructor time rather than tuition policy, which might be an understandable (but mistaken) assumption made by U.S. readers. One additional advantage to Rumble's list is the inclusion of costs to students, including real costs as well as opportunity costs. This inclusion is important, as other costing schemes ignore costs borne by others and thus ignore the higher and higher costs off-loaded to students as computer and Internet service provider (ISP) charges.

With the information about delivery costs now added to that of development costs, we can ask how the higher costs of development can be justified. In fact, it is during delivery of the online course or program that the higher investment in development begins to pay off. It does so through three mechanisms. First, technology and intelligent instructional design can substitute for higher-cost labor (the substitution of capital for labor), and second, they can also aid in the substitution of lower-cost labor for higher-cost labor (Massy and Zemsky, 1995). Research studies that specifically address these issues are included in the next chapter, specifically in the sections about faculty and instructional design.

Jewett (2000) provides a different example of this relationship. After costing online or distributed education in the California state university system, Jewett produced the graph shown in Figure 4, where the slope of the "distributed inst" line reflects the slower increase of costs attributable to the cost of interaction and evaluation (through additional instructor salaries) but not the duplicative cost of preparation and presentation time, which was designed into distributed education at the development stage. In other words, the lower cost of delivery results from decisions made about how faculty time would best be used.

The third mechanism is certainly related to the first but deserves a separate mention. With intelligent instructional design and an investment in technology, online learning can be more scalable, moving from twenty to two hundred to two thousand or more students and avoiding the necessity of building new buildings and hiring more professors at the same rate as before (McClure, 1997). Note that economies of scale ("scalability") do not imply that all two thousand students must be in one class or section; scalability can also result from repeated offerings of the course. Scalability allows development costs to be spread over more students. Although the mega-universities have used this approach, U.S. universities have been more reluctant or unable to do so. Talk about scalability, however, does not mean that no additional costs are incurred, as instructional staff must be directed toward the delivery phase of the course (for interaction and evaluation purposes), nor that there will not be other drains on the institution, including on the network, Internet access, or the course management system. In other words, scalability is not free. Research on the role of students (on whom scalability depends) is discussed in greater detail in the next chapter.

The Cost of Administration: Transforming the Business of Higher Education

Rumble's cost categories to be allocated to administration (2001) include costs that support both development and delivery but are difficult to apportion in a reasonable manner between the stages. They also support the entire institution and can include some costs we have been calling "overhead." These twenty categories are described in Table 3. Two modest revisions were made to Rumble's comprehensive list of categories. First, several categories were collapsed

Table 3
Costs of Administration

Expenditure	Description
Decision making	Includes development of an IT or distance learning or online learning strategy
Expenses related to high-level decision making	Includes travel to study other institutions, costs of consultants to help advise the institution on its online learning planning
Institutional evaluation and quality assurance	Includes staff time and expenses such as survey costs, report production, and dissemination
Web site development costs	Includes staff time and Internet specialists, graphics designer, Internet designer
Web site development support	Includes staff computers, software, and repair for individuals devoted to Web site development
Web site implementation	Includes portion of network services and maintenance as well as domain name registration
Learning platform software or course management system	Includes cost of purchase or licensing fees and costs to upgrade equipment
Learning platform or course management system equipment and costs	Includes network server, network costs, and access to the Internet, which increases with enrollment and courses offered

Table 3
(*Continued*)

Expenditure	Description
Buildings and accommodation capital costs	Includes purchase of land, construction of new building, purchase of existing building, refurbishment of existing building, rental of offices; costs depend on number of staff to be housed
Buildings and accommodation operating costs	Includes taxes paid; insurance, heat, light, water, power, waste disposal, telephone, fax, repairs and maintenance; grounds and gardens, security, cleaning, and supervision of these activities
Intranet costs	Includes computers, installing network connections, servers and server software, other software
Intranet start-up costs	Includes design consultants or in-house designers and technical support staff, training costs
Intranet ongoing costs	Includes editorial and design staff, technical personnel, ongoing consultants, promotion, training, and maintenance of applications
Furniture	Includes dedicated staff workstations and shared workstations
Local training center	Includes accommodation costs, equipment (server, computers, printers, photocopier, telephone), furnishings (desks, chairs, storage cupboards, shelving), wiring, and Internet access
Local training center staffing and consumables	Includes staff time and benefits; paper, printer cartridges, and so on
Equipment and equipment replacement	Includes insurance and simple depreciation
Digitized courseware and library	Includes cost of purchase, lease, or fee use of digitized content; library support, including staff to create and maintain records; document scanning, indexation and equipment; maintenance and repair of equipment
Marketing costs and expenses	Includes staff salaries, benefits, and consumables
Shared central costs	Includes cost of staff in human resources, purchasing, financial management, accounting, auditing, et cetera

SOURCE: Rumble, 2001, pp. 93–96.

because readers will quickly get the picture of what needs to be included; second, the term "course management system" was added to "learning platform." "Course management system" is a term more U.S. readers will recognize as equivalent to Blackboard, WebCT, or other packages that simplify the development and delivery of online instruction.

One cost that is embedded in Rumble's categories is the cost of transferring services to the Web or the development, testing, and coordination of e-services. Green (2002a) collects annual information from institutions on the types of e-services they offer; in 2002, 40.5 percent could process credit card payments (up from 27.6 percent in 2001 and 18.6 percent in 2000). A total of 70.9 percent of institutions offered online course registration (up from 55.4 percent in 2001, 43.1 percent in 2000, and 29.9 percent in 1998). As Green noted, there had been "significant gains on a number of key eCommerce and eService measures" (p. 2). And although higher education is still "roughly two years behind" (p. 3) the consumer and corporate sectors in the implementation of e-services, institutions have made substantial progress (perhaps because of, in part, their online courses and Web-savvy students). Tied to the provision of e-services is the installation of enterprise resource planning (ERP) projects that require the integration of databases across the institution, including data on students, finances, and human resources. More than 60 percent of institutions responding to the most recent Educause survey named ERP systems their number three issue (Maltz, DeBlois, and the Educause Current Issues Committee, 2005), requiring time and resources to coordinate the development and implementation of the various functions. The hope of these systems is that students who take online courses or simply access university resources online will be better and more efficiently served. Of course, these systems incur costs, including many hours of staff time to design, develop, and revise software for the database and to consult with various university functions or offices affected by the ERP, fees for consultants, testing and revision, training users, and the substantial lost time during transition and training. The cost of developing these services is large, but the promise of lower administrative costs is tantalizing.

Another cost embedded in Rumble's category of decision making is the cost of institutional research offices and personnel who are responsible for assessing technology integration, academic assessment, cost and quality of information technology services, and management and assessment of the institution's information systems (Katz and Rudy, 1999; Foster, 2001). Katz and Rudy (1999) emphasize the importance of ongoing research and planning so that resources are wisely used and align with the institution's mission.

Another clarification assumed in Rumble's work is the high fluctuation in costs resulting from continual changes in the cost of hardware and telecommunications (Moonen, 1997). Especially if these functions are leased or the institution cannot plan for or control costs imposed on them by providers, they are difficult to plan for and to cost.

What research is available on administration? As mentioned earlier, including the library in an estimate of costs to be covered under administration is extremely important. Interestingly, it is through the library that delivery and administrative costs may decline. Montgomery and King (2002) note that electronic journals are more cost-effective per use, which recognizes that they do not require the storage space of bound journals. Drexel University found, when the library went to all electronic journals, that electronic journals cost less in terms of space, more for systems (including servers, workstations, and maintenance), and more for staff (except for staff needed to bind, label, and shelve bound journals). In other words, despite some initial and ongoing costs that are higher for staff and infrastructure, the saved space and lower cost per use ($2 for electronic journals and $17.50 for print journals) more than justify the move to electronic journals. These resources are also more available and more likely to be used, a benefit to students and the educational process.

Leach and Smallen (1998, 2000) have tackled the costing of IT services, more particularly the cost of outsourcing such services as network services, helpdesk, administrative information systems, and computer repair. Institutions participating in the COSTS project provide data on their services and their costs; the database allows an institution to see whether its costs are in the middle range (between the twenty-fifth and seventy-fifth percentiles) or if its costs are very low or very high. The results showed a differential benefit, depending on the size of the institution (number of individuals, workstations, students to be supported), although some overhead was necessary to keep in-house the provision of basic functions. Therefore, economies of scale seem to be a factor in the decision to outsource some support functions and may also be influenced by the institution's sense of mission and willingness to outsource some of its functions.

Course management systems (CMSs) have been an increasingly important and pressing cost to institutions. In the Educause list of the top ten IT concerns for 2003, CMSs were ranked number nine and likely to be of greater concern as licensing fees increase (Crawford and Rudy, 2003); moreover, upgrading systems demands more or better servers and cost of time for faculty and staff to learn new skills and revise courses. In fact, several higher education systems (Wisconsin, Minnesota, North Dakota, for example) have opted to change their CMS packages, hoping to standardize all courses on one product and adopt a lower-cost product. Unfortunately, switching products is a cost, including the loss of materials during transition between packages or the lack of a transition function (the new CMS may not offer a way to transition courses from the old product to the new one). In either case, the faculty must learn, reenter, and redesign the course in the new package (Smart and Meyer, 2005), which has a distinct cost attached to it.

Bates (2000b) and Morgan (2000) would add another category to Rumble's list: the time to get academic approval of the online course or program. Although each institution, system, or state may have a procedure for gaining authorization to offer the online program, the cost of gaining this approval is likely to be variable, as it involves faculty, chairs, deans, provosts, and even presidents in lobbying for the addition or explaining what is being proposed or educating board members on the new venture. Although this expenditure of staff time may never drop to zero, it is hoped it will decline over time as approval of online programs becomes routine and is subjected to less doubt, evaluation, and justification.

The payoff depends on assumptions made during costing. Bartolic-Zlomislic and Bates (1999) report on cost-benefit analyses conducted on three Canadian telelearning projects. One of them, the University of British Columbia postgraduate certificate program in technology-based distributed learning, planned for and achieved a smaller-than-expected profit, largely the result of greater start-up costs than originally planned. The budget included overhead calculations for the continuing education division but did not include overhead for the university administration. In any case, the costs mirror the experience with so many other programs, with higher development costs but the potential for breakeven (or crossover) at some point, depending on the costing method. Wentling and Park (2001) analyzed cost for a mixed-model program at the University of Illinois at Urbana-Champaign but did not include development or overhead. Bishop and SchWeber (2001) prepared a cost analysis for an M.B.A. program at University of Maryland University College (UMUC), including overhead. The UMUC budget included an estimate of the number of student enrollments that would allow costs to be recouped and revenues to exceed costs; actual enrollment exceeded the breakeven point, as might be reasonable for an M.B.A. program. Figure 5 pictures the $334,543 UMUC budget (Carr, 2001) for the twenty-two months of the M.B.A. program and captures the costs of overhead (Web administration, administrative overhead, IT helpdesk, and program coordinator). These examples make the point that several issues must be decided when preparing budgets or costing for online programs that may be

FIGURE 5
Breakdown of UMUC Budget for M.B.A. Program

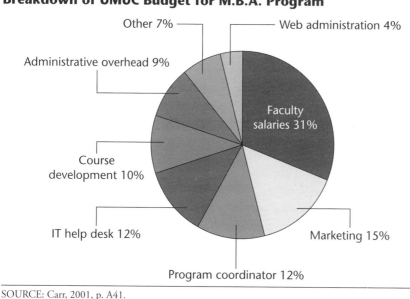

SOURCE: Carr, 2001, p. A41.

valid for a particular institution but that their results cannot easily and straight-forwardly be compared with others.

Another issue that is pertinent to costing makes more sense to the reader at this juncture of the discussion: how to apportion overhead costs from general administration to an online course or program. In other words, these overhead costs may be assessed based on the online offering's percentage of institutional student credit-hours (SCHs) generated, student contact hours, student headcount, or other formula that makes sense to the institution and its type or range of services and programs. And it may be that some overhead costs (general administration, for example) should be assessed based on SCHs and other costs (such as student services) assessed on student headcount. Student use of many student services is essentially the same whether that student is taking one three-credit class or a full credit load. In any case, this important decision must be consistent with the institution's profile and values, and no hard-and-fast rule is suitable for all institutions.

Cautions and Other Necessary Points

The literature also contains some important cautions about costing. Bacsich and Ash (1999) make an excellent case for recognizing the "barriers to costing" (pp. 3–4), including (1) the reluctance of many members (including faculty, staff, and administrators) of the organization to use a detailed time sheet, (2) the reluctance of administrators to acknowledge that staff and faculty work "overtime" and that an hourly cost or wage therefore probably does not capture the accurate cost of their time, (3) the inconsistency and nongranularity of internal accounting systems, and (4) worries that the institution's current accounting schemes could not be adapted to Activity-Based Costing. Although the authors write about their experience with universities in the United Kingdom, readers in U.S. institutions will likely recognize their own institutions in this list of barriers.

Bacsich and Ash (1999) also remark about the "cost of costing" (p. 4). In fact, the enterprise of costing does take staff time, usually an inordinate amount of time during the early stages, although it is likely that as expertise is gained with the issues and accounting procedures are adjusted, the cost may decline. In any case, the cost of costing is not something an institution can ignore. Neither can the institution ignore the "cost of having done the costing" (p. 4); that is, once the costs are identified, institutions are forced to deal with them. Even though the ignorance of costs has a cost, knowing the costs demands that action be taken or changes be made. And Bacsich and Ash (1999) worry that once costs are known, innovation will be inhibited.

Bacsich and Ash (1999) and Rumble (2001) point out that most studies of costs are conducted by institutions and do not fairly or completely incorporate the hidden costs of students. Students may be required to pay technology fees to their institution, purchase their own computers and printers, buy and upgrade software regularly, pay monthly fees to connect to an Internet service provider, purchase paper to print articles or other class-related materials, purchase inkjet cartridges to do the printing, and expend time and energy learning new skills. On the other side of the equation, studies may mention that students are avoiding costs, such as the cost of travel, parking, and car maintenance, which are incurred by commuting to a campus. But in any case, some questions remain largely unanswered by the studies included in this review: What are the total and average costs to students, and are these costs prohibitive? Do these costs add to the so-called digital divide, or are they acceptable, as the growing number of enrollments in distance education courses seems to indicate? (National Center for Education Statistics, 2002a, 2002b). In other words, let us stop inferring that the enrollment data mean costs are acceptable and ask students what additional costs are acceptable to them and which students cannot participate because of the increased costs.

Ash (2000) provides a balance to these concerns. She stresses the importance of including costing efforts in a larger approach to evaluating the effectiveness of online learning. Her point is that universities should be "cost-aware"; that is, each "action, decision and outcome is treated in a cost-aware manner" (p. 2). Costing should be embedded in the university's culture and operation, not a separate exercise to evaluate one activity and not the entire enterprise. This approach places cost-aware decision making in the context of evaluation that is integral to the university's ongoing, day-to-day operations (p. 6). Evaluation should judge the viability of the innovation, such as online learning programs, in terms of the users and all the stakeholders. Ash (2000) also points out that the only way innovations such as online learning can be relieved of the charge that the Hawthorne Effect (whereby students achieve more in an online setting solely because they are being studied and feel special) is the cause for better outcomes is when evaluation is an everyday activity for *all* activities (p. 6).

These cautions are not sufficient to keep an institution from investigating the costs of online learning, but doing so has some disadvantages that the institution also needs to keep in mind. It may be that the costing exercise will provide the type of data the institution needs to make wiser decisions regarding use of resources, or it may stifle innovation, generate pressures to use cost data in a simplistic way, or only raise further and more profound barriers to the costing enterprise. Whether costing is used to stifle or stimulate online learning is up to the institution's leaders and the organization's mission and values. Institutions can also adopt a cost-aware approach to all decision making and make evaluation of *all* activities a priority, which will likely ensure that online learning is not singled out unfairly or held to higher standards than other higher education activities.

This chapter has reviewed existing research and thinking on the elements of the framework, drawing heavily on Rumble (2001) but including many other cost studies. The careful reader may have wondered about missing information or still have questions about each element. The last two chapters discuss the implications of the current research and the questions that remain after our review. But before we can define implications or research questions, the next chapter tackles a review of the research on the seven factors in the framework: students, faculty, other staff, instructional design, content, infrastructure, and policy.

Research on the Factors
of Online Learning

THIS CHAPTER FOCUSES ON THE RESEARCH and other literature that have been collected and categorized into the seven factors:
students, faculty, other staff, instructional design, content, infrastructure, and
policy. It tries to identify how each factor affects cost-efficiency, how it may
interact with the elements and other factors, and what we do not yet know
about the factor or its interactions.

Students Are Key

Research on or about students may be the most plentiful of all the factors,
with the exception of faculty. The literature tends to group its focus on six
qualities of students, however: their numbers, their propensity to finish or
drop out, their motivation and ability to learn online, supporting them online,
costs to students, and benefits to students.

First, many studies and writers have stressed the importance of student
numbers: their ability, through enrolling in one large course or the same course
over several semesters, to help institutions achieve economies of scale. For
example, Bartolic-Zlomislic and Bates (1999) documented how a postgraduate certificate program broke even at the end of three years of offering the
program, which is a good example of how one achieves economies of scale
with smaller annual numbers of students but repetition of the coursework.
Bishop (2002) documented how Riverside Community College redesigned
an elementary algebra course that enrolled thirty-six hundred students annually and Pennsylvania State University redesigned its elementary statistics

course that enrolled twenty-two hundred students annually. Perhaps the best examples of how student numbers affect cost-efficiency are the mega-universities, which enroll 2.8 million students at a cost of around $350 per student (Daniel, 1997).

But an institution need not be a mega-university to benefit from economies of scale. A large number of students interested in one course is especially important to offset the higher cost of developing online courses, but this condition clearly applies to few courses. Just twenty-five courses generate about half of all student enrollments in community colleges and a third of all enrollments at four-year institutions (Twigg, 2003a). Twigg's Program in Course Redesign was originally developed to target high-enrollment courses in particular, such as introductory mathematics courses, general education courses such as sociology 101, or courses that are particularly problematic for students but are crucial to their entering certain programs such as chemistry 101. But it is also important that enrollments be stable, which is another argument for redesigning general education or required courses. Although these studies are reviewed more fully in the section on instructional design, it is important to note that redesigning higher-enrollment courses allows the cost of the redesign to be recouped and also benefits more students.

Certificate programs are another way to achieve higher enrollments (Bartolic-Zlomislic and Bates, 1999; Robinson, 2001). This observation assumes that the course has wider appeal or is marketable to several populations rather than be of interest to a few. Of course, it is possible to aggregate a lower number of scattered students into a certificate program.

But large numbers need not always be extremely large. Bates (2000b) notes that at the University of British Columbia (UBC), as "numbers per class increase beyond forty per year over a four-year period," it becomes more cost-effective to invest in developing Web-based courses, assuming that "interaction between students and teachers remains high" (p. 128). UBC avoids developing online courses for fewer than twenty students per year. But for courses that enroll between twenty and forty students a year, "cost differences are likely to be less significant than differences in benefits" (p. 129) in terms of student learning. Bates also clarifies that the institution must look at the life of the course: "each time the course is offered, the average cost per student comes down, so the life of the course, or the number of times it is offered, is significant" (2000b, p. 144). Two important points can be gleaned from these observations. First, as Arvan and others (1998) also stress, it is important to determine the number of semesters it would take to recover development costs for a course; institutions need to calculate this number so that they can make informed decisions about which course to develop and how much to invest in its development. Second, rather than focusing only on introductory courses or high-enrollment courses, Bates provides a good argument for incorporating some higher-development online applications in smaller courses as long as they can be repeated several times without revision and the cost of development is not too extravagant.

Note that this discussion has not been about determining the optimum number of students for e-learning programs. Bates (2000b) states that the appropriate number of students should be influenced by educational philosophy, course design, and available technology. Size is therefore not to be determined solely by concerns about cost-efficiency, but once size and development costs have been estimated, the institution can determine the point at which the development costs can reasonably be recovered.

Jewett (2000) takes another look at the importance of numbers, with a view toward designing mediated learning labs, more particularly a lab for remedial mathematics. Small (twenty students) and medium (thirty students) labs were always higher in cost than regular classroom instruction. Only when the lab was large (fifty or more) could the cost of adding another section finally achieve a lower cost than the classroom option at around one thousand annual student enrollments. This finding can guide investments in designing online or mediated courses, and whether (and how) a campus can provide computer lab courses in a cost-efficient manner. A study by Harley, Maher, Henke, and Lawrence (2003) found that redesigning an introductory chemistry course allowed for some reduction of time spent in labs, which could allow for greater student enrollments in the course as more lab sections are added. These studies clearly indicate that mediated learning can increase the use of such limited physical resources as labs.

Second, data are conflicting on the retention or dropout rates of students in online learning. Some attrition is normal, of course, but how much?

Brigham (2003) found 66 percent of distance-learning institutions had an 80 percent or better completion rate for their distance-learning courses; 87 percent of these institutions had a 70 percent or better completion rate. Jung and Leem (in Jung and Rha, 2000) found that an online course had a higher completion rate (93.1 percent) than a traditional, text-and-television distance education course (55.25 percent). It is likely that some of the early rates of attrition were higher because of the course's poor design. Twigg's projects on course redesign (2003a) focused on improving course retention over an earlier, traditional version of the same course. These projects improved the drop-failure-withdrawal rate from 28 percent to 19 percent in introductory psychology at the University of Southern Maine, from 49 percent to 38 percent in computer programming at Drexel University, from 45 percent to 11 percent in fine arts at Florida Gulf Coast University, and from 39 percent to 25 percent in introductory sociology at Indiana University–Purdue University Indianapolis.

Third, advocates have promoted online learning because it can make constructivist learning a reality (Diaz, 2000; Brown, 1998). The Web is a rich place well suited for students to make connections, construct meaning, navigate subjects, and create their own knowledge. These possibilities change the paradigm for students, away from passive learning to active learning, requiring that they take greater responsibility for making time for and taking effort with their learning. Given that much online learning requires students be more involved and more autonomous in their learning, are students ready and motivated to learn in this fashion? Morgan (2000), Finkelstein and Scholz (2000), and Bartolic-Zlomislic and Bates (1999) asked this question; an answer might only be temporary as students continue to change, or it may apply only to some younger students and not to adult students (or vice versa), or it may apply just to some students who have been and may always be a portion of the student population. "The very needy students who need constant reassurance need constant direction" (Bartolic-Zlomislic and Bates, 1999, p. 15), and such students may not learn well online. This concern about readiness to learn online seems to fly in the face of the popular characterization of students as "digital natives" and faculty as "digital immigrants" (Prensky, 2001; VanSlyke, 2003). These terms seem to imply that students are naturals in the digital world, so why might they not be equally at home in the online class? Perhaps despite their digital expertise, their earlier learning has stressed passive learning or an instructivist philosophy. It is an interesting quandary and one worth understanding much better than we do today. If current enrollments in online programs of almost 1 million are any indication, however, some students have voted with their feet. But this factor is only part of the equation, because if they are not ready to learn in ways that online learning makes possible, it may exacerbate problems with retention, thereby lowering cost-efficiencies.

Rumble (n.d.) points out another way that students may add to the costs of online learning. "The biggest and . . . least costed ingredient in the costs of on-line learning is the cost of supporting learners online" (p. 4). This point is intriguing, because it apparently applies to learners who are new to online learning but also to learners who—although experienced—may experience novel technical and operational difficulties or a steep learning curve whenever new software packages (such as course management systems) or new equipment is acquired. It is important not to underestimate the time demands on faculty or other assistants of addressing these problems, which can range from thirty minutes to four hours per student per week (Arizona Learning Systems, 1998, p. 22). This demand for learning support argues for restricting course enrollments or providing ongoing technical assistance. The demand on instructors for learning support would also increase for students who are unsuited for independent learning or require more one-on-one attention to keep them motivated or prevent them from giving up when faced with a technical problem. Despite these cost demands, however, learning support may be one of the crucial elements for keeping students enrolled, thereby lowering the dropout rate.

Several writers have focused on how online learning can help students avoid the costs (gasoline, auto depreciation, time) of commuting (Finkelstein and Scholz, 2000, p. 19). Bacsich and Ash (1999) believe that students increasingly behave as though time has an opportunity cost and that time saved in commuting may be available for work, study, or family. For employers, online education represents less travel for their employees and less time away from work (American Management Association, 2003a, 2003b).

On the other hand, students bear additional costs: technology fees, a computer and printer, software and software upgrades, an ISP connection (Eggins, 2000, p. 68; Rumble, n.d.). Bishop (2002) describes another increased cost for students: requiring that they take a tutorial on online learning, which requires a course fee (p. 180), although Morgan (2000) insists that such a tutorial may help improve retention and student satisfaction (or weed out those students for whom online learning is not a good fit). Given the growth of technology use by all students, however, these new costs are likely borne by all higher education students, be they online or on campus. Indeed, proper equipment to access the Internet is either provided by some few institutions (the "laptop colleges") or assumed to be standard student preparation for college by many others. In fact, 42.5 percent of postsecondary institutions in 1998 required students to pay technology fees (Green, 1998), a figure that has likely increased since then. This observation confirms that additional costs are not borne solely by students in online courses but by nearly all students studying at U.S. colleges and universities.

Last, many examples exist of how students may benefit from online learning: increased access to different types of education or programs, increased access to more courses and more variety in courses, and better and easier access to learning resources (such as electronic journals) (Finkelstein and Scholz, 2000). Moonen (1997) mentions that student time is often ignored as a cost, but it is not clear whether students invest more time on learning, increasing their time on task, or less time as a result of "more effective structure of the learning materials and the better organization of the instructional process" (p. 6). Certainly, when asked, students mention convenience and flexibility as a reason to enroll in online courses, allowing them to take courses when they want rather than when the university can offer them, which benefits working adults as much as students enrolled on campus. Unfortunately, it is difficult to figure out how to assign a cost to these benefits, and therefore they are often lost in the focus on and calculations of cost-efficiencies. Moreover, if online courses help students finish their degree faster or sooner, then the institution can enroll new students to take their place, helping the state serve more students and provide more access to higher education with existing resources. This list is not meant to ignore the learning benefits to students, which are extremely important, but are outside the immediate purview of this report. In any case these benefits to students and the assertion that online coursework can help students progress through their studies more efficiently, thereby opening enrollment spaces for new students, require further documentation.

Faculty Are Essential

The role of faculty in online learning has attracted the greatest number of studies in the literature. Faculty are an important resource for postsecondary education, perhaps the most essential resource for carrying out the work of teaching students, researching new knowledge, and providing service to various communities. Faculty time is perhaps the institution's most constrained resource; Massy (2003) calls faculty time the university's "scarcest resource" (p. 260), which argues for using faculty time with an eye to its best and highest use.

When the issue is putting courses and programs online, faculty play an essential role in developing and rethinking online courses and ensuring that students learn as much or more than before. Their cooperation is crucial for another reason: as institutions grapple with stagnant budget growth, they are an essential partner in the attempt to use resources as efficiently as possible. Because college and university budgets are often reserved primarily for salaries of personnel (averaging 80 to 90 percent of the total budget), greater efficiency is usually translated into more or different teaching. Therefore, for institutions to reap efficiencies from the salaries paid to faculty, they must have the active cooperation of faculty as the faculty role is rethought, revised, and transformed. The following studies can be grouped into six topics: increased time commitments of faculty involved in online education, replacing capital for labor, replacing faculty with lower-cost labor, transformation of the faculty role, faculty as barriers to change, and the advantages to be accrued from the faculty learning curve.

Perhaps the largest number of studies confirms that online learning demands additional time on the part of faculty. Studies by Geith (2003), the National Education Association (NEA) (2000), Geith and Cometa (1999), the National Center for Education Statistics (2002a), Bartolic-Zlomislic and Bates (1999), Bartolic-Zlomislic and Brett (1999), and Eggins (2000) identify the greater time commitment of faculty as one of the usual side effects of including more technology in teaching or moving coursework online. The NEA survey of members (2000) found that most faculty do spend more time on their distance courses than their traditional courses, and 84 percent do not get a reduced workload to handle the greater time commitment. The National Center for Education Statistics (2002a, p. v) found that faculty teaching distance education courses actually had a higher teaching load (which may reflect the higher teaching loads at community colleges, where much distance education has occurred). In addition, faculty who teach distance education courses had higher average office hours and hours spent on e-mail from students per week (National Center for Education Statistics, 2002a, p. vi). An evaluation of online courses at the University of Toronto by Bartolic-Zlomislic and Brett (1999) found that the largest cost of the course was for tutoring and grading, the result of choosing to use online discussions and a more constructivist philosophy for the course. Meyer (forthcoming) has found that assessing online discussions requires an enormous commitment of time from faculty. Moonen (1997) found that instructors received thirty to one hundred e-mail messages per day, which means that in a class of sixty to one hundred twenty students who each send one e-mail that requires five minutes to respond, the extra time needed to handle e-mail is five to ten hours per week (p. 5). These studies should not be taken as an argument for eliminating e-mail between students and faculty or using a less constructivist approach to student learning, as interaction with faculty is essential to student learning and constructivism is a powerful approach that encourages and retains student learning. Because e-mail impacts faculty workload, however, it demands that faculty find sound pedagogical ways to address students' needs without answering each e-mail individually or spending an inordinate amount of time on grading. In fact, too many e-mails may be a sign of poorly designed instruction that is still instructor-centric. New techniques for managing interaction in a class depend on having students help each other first and going to faculty only with unresolved questions, which builds community in the class, improves student learning, and avoids exhausting faculty.

The additional time commitment for faculty is spent in a variety of ways besides answering e-mails. Bartolic-Zlomislic and Bates (1999) identified a rapid learning curve for faculty in its three case studies of online programs that include time to learn the software to be used, designing courses, and providing online instruction. Eggins (2000), in the context of cost studies in the United Kingdom, specifically mentions the additional time spent by faculty to learn new technologies, integrate computer-based materials into classes, and develop new course materials. Rumble (n.d.) noted that additional time was needed for faculty training and the development of materials. McClure (1997) provides this comprehensive overview of the time demands on faculty to learn and the "faculty learning barrier:"

> *Enabling current university faculty to create and participate in a student-centered electronic learning environment requires our investment in technology, design, pedagogical change, and personal change. Most obviously, we must become fluent in using technologies that have not been entirely within our experience while our students grew up with them. We have to learn a whole new approach to instructional design. Designing a course to be delivered at a blackboard and designing a course to be delivered collaboratively and interactively across a network are very different things. Professors have to learn new pedagogical models and ways of interacting with students [p. 8].*

Not all faculty have as much to learn, however. Green (2002b) argues that the faculty now entering academe began their academic careers as freshmen in 1984, the first cohort of aspiring academics who experienced computers as a part of their academic experience from its beginning. Unfortunately, classroom instruction seems the same as in 1984, with few exceptions. Yet this note is positive in some regards. Younger faculty may be more open to the use of computers and more experienced with using the Web in instruction. So the learning curve for faculty described by McClure (1997) may not apply in its entirety to the young faculty described by Green (2002b), although studies that address these generational differences of faculty are missing from the literature.

Let us turn now to the issue of how much time it actually takes to develop an online course. Based on the work of Rumble (1997), Boettcher reports the following estimates of faculty work to produce one hour of student learning using different "technologies":

Lecture: 2–10 hours

Small group teaching: 1–10 hours

Videotaped lectures: 3–10 hours

Teaching text (book): 50–100 hours

Broadcast television: 100 hours

Computer-aided learning: 200 hours

Interactive learning (could include computer simulation, animation, digital video): 300 hours [Boettcher, 2004, p. 5].

Based on these data, Boettcher concludes that eighteen hours to develop one hour of student learning on the Web seems "about right" (2004, p. 5). These estimates of time required to produce Web-based student learning are based on solid guidelines and experience, and they confirm faculty perceptions and institution experience that developing online courses takes more time than developing traditional courses.

Another interesting insight into faculty perception that online courses take more of their time is the work of Geith and Vignare (2001) and Geith and Cometa (1999). These studies found that all faculty felt they spent more time when teaching online courses. But when the researchers investigated the faculty's self-reported hours, only three of the nine online sections actually consumed more faculty time per student than more traditional courses. Five sections consumed about the same amount of faculty time, and one section consumed less time. On the other hand, Hislop (2001a) had four faculty complete time logs while teaching two courses each—one online and one face-to-face—with both requiring the same curriculum. Instructional time did not differ much (333 hours online versus 347 hours in the face-to-face class), but the online courses did take more time per student, and interactions with students were spread out over more days in the week, not just on the days when the class met (Hislop, 2001a). Studies by Geith and her colleagues would have us believe that faculty perceptions of how much time it takes to teach online are not reliable, but Hislop claims that faculty perceptions of time may be more credible when the analysis breaks down total time spent per student or other analyses. Or it may be that faculty perceptions about time spent online are different because patterns of behavior are different from earlier experiences. Clearly, this area requires further study.

The increase in demands placed on faculty time is offset somewhat by the decreased time faculty must spend in research or to prepare classes. "Electronic access to materials, instant communication among scholars, online journals, electronic publishing, or review of articles in traditional journals via the Internet are among the many ways in which IT is saving researchers time and labor and making their work more efficient" (Finkelstein and Scholz, 2000, pp. 16–17). IT increases *individual* productivity for students, faculty, and administrators through greater efficiencies in research and writing (p. 20). But it is not the same as *instructional* productivity or *administrative* productivity, which are discussed elsewhere in this report.

Moreover, many studies on faculty deal with what economists call the "replacement of capital for labor" or the use of technology to lessen the use of faculty. No study makes a case that faculty could or would be replaced by technology, but they do identify ways that the Web could perform some functions previously done by faculty. Instead, the focus has been on the transformation of what is characterized as a "handicraft" tradition (Massy, 2002), where each faculty crafts the course for each offering, to an industrial production model, where instruction is standardized and more students are enrolled. This transformation is not exactly the same as what is meant by "unbundling" the faculty role, whereby traditional faculty duties are now performed by others who are more expert at assessment, course development, or some other duty (Jones and Matthews, 2002; Oblinger, 1999). In any case, Massy is emphatic that "technology can't replace the human factor in education. It can leverage faculty labor, but it can't replace it" (Massy, 2002, p. 5). Faculty labor can be leveraged through wise use of online course design and use of their skills and knowledge in ways that help students learn.

With these provisos in mind, let us summarize five primary methods by which capital is used to substitute for labor. First, faculty have traditionally been characterized as the holder of content, which is transmitted to students through lecturing or the curriculum embedded in the class. With the advent of the Web and high-speed connections, however, it is now possible for the content held by faculty to be delivered in a traditional fashion—with a lecture—but made available at any time that is convenient to the student to view or hear over the Web. Second, rather than having content available solely in textbooks or libraries, digitization of content means it is increasingly available on the Web for students to access. Third, the design of a course can be duplicated by software, such as can be found in course management systems. Fourth, learning exercises can be developed that use the software to teach, such as drill and practice or simulations. Fifth, to the extent that assessment and testing can be automated into the software, students can test their knowledge and the institution can ensure that the learning intended has occurred. These are all examples of tasks that have traditionally been within the purview of faculty but have now been designed into the course. Capital (in this case, the hardware and software that captures faculty expertise in content, pedagogy, and testing) has replaced the labor of faculty. More examples of this process are discussed in the review of studies on instructional design. Each method is a means of transforming the faculty role (discussed in more detail later in this section).

Another large group of studies deals with ways to substitute lower-cost labor (part-time faculty, graduate assistants, peer tutors) for higher-cost faculty labor. One way is to use the "train the trainer" approach (American Management Association, 2003a) popular in business and education; it uses faculty time for the initial training but less expensive labor for additional training. Pennsylvania State University, for example, uses a teaching associate to allow faculty to handle larger numbers of students. The Open University has invested heavily in well-trained part-time tutors, where the ratio of full-time to part-time academic staff is one to nine (Finkelstein and Scholz, 2000, p. 19).

In each of these examples, tasks traditionally performed by faculty are designed so that they can be done by the technology, the course design embedded in the technology, or lower-cost labor. The important point is that one does not simply replace faculty with a graduate assistant but that some design or use of technology captures faculty expertise in the design and content but frees up faculty time spent on some activities and allocates those activities to lower-cost labor. For example, graduate assistants or part-time faculty can ably respond to basic student questions such as might occur in introductory courses and where individuals are available who have this knowledge. Further, lower-cost labor may be just as capable to perform some assessment tasks—such as evaluating online discussions with a rubric or providing grammatical or writing feedback on a paper—which would free up faculty time for performing higher-level assessments. (More examples are found in the studies reviewed in the section on instructional design.)

For example, faculty costs (including time for course development and delivery) accounted for much of the difference in cost between an asynchronous course and an on-campus course. Without redesigning the course, faculty costs accounted for 69 percent of the costs of the asynchronous course and 41 percent of the on-campus course (Geith and Cometa, 1999), supporting the argument for finding ways to use faculty time more efficiently or using lower-cost labor at appropriate places in the course.

Several influential writers focus on how information technology is transforming the faculty role. "The faculty role will change from being mainly a content expert . . . to a combination of content expert, learning process design expert, and process implementation manager. Faculty will also be motivators and mentors, interpreters (especially of non-codified knowledge), and, as a colleague recently put it, 'expert learners'—people who lead the learning process by breaking trail and setting the right personal example. Technology can leverage faculty time, but it cannot replace most human contact without significant quality losses" (Massy, 2002, pp. 5–6).

But faculty are not the only holders of content knowledge; much content knowledge can be captured on the Web and in texts. In fact, Daniel (1997) believes that content will be less important than accessing, sharing, and creating new knowledge, which is where faculty expertise can best be applied. When courses are redesigned to use information technology to free up faculty time, faculty may then focus on their "highest and best uses. By shifting many of the routine and repetitive aspects of teaching and student evaluation to the technology, faculty will be able to concentrate on the kinds of intellectual questions that represent their comparative advantages" (Massy, 2002, p. 14). This thought is similar to those found in Geith (2003) and Graves (1994), who hypothesized that faculty could be freed up from some tasks (such as lecturing) to spend more time on the sort of "in-depth contact between subject expert and a small group of learners . . . [that] is at the heart of our nation's peerless reputation in higher education" (Graves, 1994, p. 36). These notions are attractive but require careful documentation to determine whether it is what is happening to the faculty role.

A few studies still focus on faculty as barriers to online learning, but this thought appears less often in more current studies. McClure (1997) mentions the role of faculty autonomy and the resulting reluctance to follow institutional needs or goals. On the other hand, many faculty have been very positive about technology, using it for many day-to-day tasks. In a 1998 survey by the National Education Association, 70 percent of faculty had a computer at home, 25 percent had been involved with distance education, and 27 percent had a Web site for their classes. And almost 90 percent believed that "student use of computers enhance their learning" (National Education Association, 2000, p. 5). These figures likely have grown since 1998. In fact, without substantial faculty interest and support, the growth in online courses from 25,730 to 127,400 in 2000–01 (see National Center for Education Statistics, 1999, 2003) would not have occurred. Thus, always characterizing faculty as a barrier to online learning is inaccurate, although individual faculty certainly will continue to raise doubts or resist the move toward online or mediated learning. Raising doubts may well be healthy and a tonic to the sometimes overstated claims of advocates (Feenberg, 1999), encouraging advocates to make a better case for uses of technology. In fact, Bates (2000b) makes the case that some of the resistance to online learning is the result of faculty's needing much more support and encouragement than have been provided in the past.

Perhaps an underlying issue in experiencing transformation of the faculty role and faculty resistance to use of technology is the erosion of faculty control over the curriculum and the classroom, over the means of delivering the curriculum, and over how the job is done (Massy and Zemsky, 1995; McClure, 1997). Massy and Zemsky (1995) call the trade-off between faculty control and educational cost—as they are affected by information technology—a Gordian knot. In other words, the only way to really save costs through online education is to cut through faculty control over the curriculum and the means of transmitting it to students. Perhaps it would be better to say that we need to refashion the role of faculty and their responsibility to the curriculum and students so that they can incorporate the institution's need to use resources wisely and well.

Faculty are essential for another reason: it is through their learning curve that methods for improving cost-efficiencies and cost-effectiveness are hypothesized, tested, learned, and improved. Massy (2002) argues that the learning curve depends on adopting the principles of continuous quality improvement, which depend on feedback systems that track student learning and allow faculty to diagnose difficulties and explore solutions. In fact, without their learning, the institution could not achieve the efficiencies it needs. Jewett and Henderson (2003) provide some evidence that "a learning curve for faculty and staff associated with converting and offering mediated courses" (p. 23) translates into reducing costs by 10 percent in the second year, 6 percent in the third, and 2 percent in the fourth, or a cumulative cost reduction of about 15 percent as "thoughtful people learn to do things better and more efficiently" (p. 23). This observation rings true, as experience brings both new knowledge and the disconfirmation of old knowledge to those who experiment with online learning. What the amount of cost reduction is, however, perhaps needs further research or long-term studies that should also confirm whether the learning curve has such an effect.

This review of the research on the role of faculty in achieving cost-efficiencies recognizes that faculty are essential to online learning. Their time and role in student learning, and their growing expertise in going online and ensuring it works well for students, are essential. In other words, online learning must have the active involvement of faculty to succeed.

Other Staff Are New Costs

In the past ten years, higher education institutions have added new staff to handle the demands of new technologies, the Web, and online learning. A partial list of these new staff includes network designers and technicians, infrastructure specialists (including intranets), instructional designers, Web designers and developers, technicians for the implementation of course management systems, database experts, software developers, and a variety of trainers on productivity software, CMS upgrades, and higher-end applications. And do not forget all the supervisors, managers, and directors who are responsible for ensuring these services are always up and running. These staff may have been the fastest-growing category of new employees at colleges and universities for several years.

Unfortunately, data from the National Center for Education Statistics are not reported in these categories. Professional staff as a proportion of total staff have grown, from 58 percent in 1976 to 65 percent in 1993 to 66 percent in 1997 (National Center for Education Statistics 1996, 2000a), but these figures include all administrators as well as faculty. If the category of staff called "technical and paraprofessional" captures at least some of these new staff, then they are only 7 percent of the staff (in 1995), growing in number from 167,377 in 1987 to 230,588 in 1991 and then falling to 187,900 in 1995 (National Center for Education Statistics, 1998). These numbers translate into increased costs. Green (2000) has indicated that between 40 and 50 percent of an institution's expenditures on information technology can be credited to personnel salaries and benefits. Therefore, it may be as appropriate to ask what efficiencies result from the addition of these personnel as have been repeatedly asked about faculty. If faculty account for only 36 percent of all professional staff (National Center for Education Statistics, 1998), then focusing solely on faculty is not sufficient to improve efficiencies or productivity. In other words, although the focus on instruction is surely an important way to improve efficiency, an institution can also focus its efforts on improving productivity on other aspects of its operation and other types of staff.

Studies by Hislop (2001b) and Miller (2001) note the higher cost of online programs, resulting in part from the addition of these important technical and design staff. Yet Green (2000) emphasizes that despite the addition of new staff, IT support at colleges and universities is well below levels found in corporations. The ratio of users to support staff on college campuses runs two to ten times higher than that found in large corporations and small businesses (p. 60). This thought is sobering, because despite the large numbers of specialized IT staff added in the past ten years, they are not being added at the levels required by the same businesspeople who claim universities are inefficient.

Yet surprisingly little attention is paid to these costs or to data on how many of these new personnel are on campus. They support a variety of functions on campus: administration, student services, academic departments, continuing education, alumni, and development. They are not a cost to be charged to online learning courses or programs in their entirety, as their services are now ubiquitous and essential to most functions of the institution. What portion (if any) of these costs might be legitimately charged to an online program is a decision that needs to be made and justified at the institutional level.

Finkelstein and Scholz (2000) point out that it is often IT professionals who replace faculty when we discuss replacing capital for labor (as in the earlier discussion on faculty). Unfortunately, many IT professionals command higher salaries than faculty, although they do not have tenure. In other words, expecting cost savings strictly from the replacement of one type of staff for faculty is inadequate; it is through the new professionals' ability to redesign the processes of instruction and learning that the potential for savings can be made a reality. This is a necessary caution against interpreting an economic process (replacing capital for labor) too simplistically, without undergoing the process of instructional redesign. It is a good example not only of the interaction between factors but also of the way that the factors must combine to create cost-efficiencies.

With regard to developing a budget for the online program, Bates (2000b) estimates that a minimum of 5 percent of the total instructional budget is needed for support staff, including technical and instructional support staff. This guideline applies not only to the online program but also (perhaps) to all other instructional programs.

It should be clear that these staff people are essential for enabling online learning as well as ensuring it is done well. Instructional design and Web experts certainly are essential for making the next factor, instructional design, a reality and for making the substitutions of capital for labor or lower-cost labor for higher-cost labor discussed earlier. In fact, it may well be said that the benefits of instructional design could not have been achieved without the efforts of these unnamed staff with their expertise in Web design, instructional design, and course management systems. This is an excellent example of an interaction between two factors or cells in the framework ("other staff" and "instructional design"), and it is a shame that so few research studies have specifically addressed this topic other than noting their absolute necessity. This area is prime for further research and study.

Instructional Design Is the Gold Mine

Instructional design appears to produce gold because it helps faculty and institutions overcome the add-on uses of technology. Instead of using technology to add activities to an existing course or duplicate processes from the traditional course in the online course (such as happens when traditional talking-head lectures are delivered online), instructional design pushes transformation. It asks whether student learning can be achieved in other, nontraditional ways; for example, the role of the lecture to deliver important content to students may be transformed to online content or modules that may include text, visuals, and audiovisual components. In fact, instructional design can "right size" learning for students, taking into consideration both student resources and constructivist learning. "Small-scale chemistry," for example, reproduces an expensive chemistry lab with inexpensive supplies or materials already in-house at much less cost to both student and institution (National Small-Scale Chemistry Center, n.d.). Instructional design also takes advantage of pedagogies that stress active learning for students and other pedagogies that have been proved to increase student learning or the retention of learning over time. In these ways, instructional design can certainly improve student learning, but it can also improve cost-efficiencies as well.

This topic will be benefited by a number of well-designed studies conducted as part of the Program in Course Redesign hosted through the National Center for Academic Transformation and led by Carol Twigg (http://www.thencat.org). Other studies will also be included from projects funded by the Mellon Foundation or the Sloan Foundation, but the bulk are the product of Twigg's effort to focus institutions on those courses where redesign could benefit more students and generate greater efficiencies for the institution. With funding from Pew Charitable Trusts, thirty institutions received grants to redesign courses accompanied by a solid plan to lower costs and document improved student learning. Those thirty institutions reduced costs an average of 37 percent (some projects reduced costs by 15 percent and others by 77 percent) and generated a savings of $3.1 million *per year* in operating costs (Twigg, 2005, p. 35). (More detailed information on the individual projects can be found at http://www.thencat.org/PCR.htm.) This section focuses on various strategies for producing these results (including the three substitutions of capital for labor, lower-cost labor for higher-cost labor, and capital for capital) and the benefits accruing from the redesign. In this instance, the term "cost-effectiveness" is more apt, as these studies documented the impact of course redesign on student learning.

Substituting Capital for Labor

Let us begin with some poor examples of replacing capital for labor. Bates (2000b) mentions such early practices as simply placing lecture notes on the Web, providing information to students through e-mail, adding a discussion forum, or putting hyperlinks to online readings in a course Web site. These practices may be improvements, but they do not represent a marked change in how faculty use their time (indeed, both examples may require faculty to spend more time finding and putting notes or links online) and neither has been linked so far to improved learning. The problem with these examples is that they are still embedded in the current paradigm, with faculty still key to the teaching enterprise. It is only when "their minds escape from that set of rules and make the leap into a totally new way of doing things" (McClure, 1997, p. 2) that radical change is possible. Substituting capital for labor is fundamental to making this leap.

How do institutions substitute capital for labor in ways that can be truly cost-efficient? Pennsylvania State University decreased the time spent on lectures and increased the use of computer-mediated instruction; the University of Central Florida used online modules; Brigham Young University used multimedia lessons; Virginia Tech created a physical math lab; Fairfield University replaced dissection labs with computer-based activities and decreased laboratory costs by 73 percent; the University of Tennessee–Knoxville reduced the cost to students of textbooks and other materials by customizing materials and offering online access to them (Twigg, 2005, 2003a, 2003b; Waddoups, Hatch, and Butterworth, 2003). Campbell and others (2004) describe the use of virtual labs to teach electronics, resulting in lower cost per student and learning as good as physical labs plus higher student satisfaction with the more flexible virtual labs. The University of Central Florida also used online quizzes to provide feedback to students; Texas A&M used an application of online quizzes that personalized problem sets, quizzes, and exams (Fisher and Nygren, 2000). Arvan and others (1998) also used online quizzes to help students assess their own learning and identify what they needed to work on. The University of Buffalo used online grading, and the use of course management systems generally reduced faculty time spent on recording, calculating, and storing grades, photocopying materials, posting changes, and sending out announcements (Twigg, 2002). Twigg (2005) estimates that if all higher education institutions in the United States redesign their top twenty-five courses, the "cost of instruction would be reduced *annually* by approximately 16 percent–while improving student learning and retention" (p. 48).

In most of these cases, faculty time was redesigned, away from lecturing and grading repetitive quizzes to developing the redesigned course; in other cases, the redesign allowed the institution to reduce the number of faculty needed to teach a course in psychology statistics from five to one (Fisher and Nygren, 2000), or numerous sections taught by different instructors could be made more consistent in content and learning outcomes (Waddoups, Hatch, and Butterworth, 2003. In the latter study, class meeting time was reduced in lieu of both multimedia lessons and one-on-one meetings with writing faculty, which reduced faculty time by 25 percent and contributed to better papers (based on evaluations by three readers) in the online sections.

A redesign can also allow an institution to make other changes. Fairfield University reduced the number of sections taught and increased the number of students in each section; Virginia Tech and the University of Southern Mississippi were also able to reduce the number of sections and increase enrollments. Pennsylvania State University reduced the number of graduate assistants in its redesigned course. The University of Illinois at Urbana-Champaign, Portland State University, and Florida Gulf Coast University increased the number of enrollments per section as a result of their redesigns, although each project included several other changes as well (see details of these changes as well as many others at http://www.thencat.org/PlanRes/R2R_CostRed.htm).

These changes are based on five principles of redesign: (1) redesign the whole course; (2) encourage active learning; (3) provide students with individualized instruction; (4) build in ongoing assessment and prompt (automated) feedback; and (5) ensure sufficient time on task and monitor students' progress (see Twigg, 2005, and http://www.thencat.org/PlanRes/R2R_PrinCR.htm). These principles are noticeably similar to Chickering and Gamson's seven principles of good practice for undergraduate instruction (1987), which are applied to online learning in greater detail in a later section. In any case, when a course is redesigned and put online, the principles for improving student learning seem to be remarkably similar to those for improving learning in traditional courses; the advantage in terms of cost-efficiency is that the redesign can also rethink how faculty time is used and make the various substitutions that can lower cost.

These substitutions work best, however, in five conditions. First, they work well when enough students take the course to justify the expenditure. It can be the twenty-five courses that account for half the student enrollments at community colleges or one-third of the enrollments at colleges (Twigg, 2003a). Second, they can be the courses that, when repeated over enough semesters, enroll enough students that also justify the expenditure of redesigning the course. Third, they can be the courses that, given their difficulty, act as a barrier to students' continuing their studies. Fourth, the course must represent a fairly stable curriculum (Miller, 2001) that will not need to be revamped and added to substantially in subsequent offerings of the course. Although modest revisions are the norm in any offering of an online course, it would be best if they were kept to a sensible minimum. Fifth, Miller (2001) mentions that "scope creep" (p. 166)—the tendency to overbuild a course and add features that are nice but not required—must be avoided. In other words, institutions pursuing this route to cost-efficiencies need to monitor their instructional design efforts so that course design and revision do not go overboard.

Massy (2002) calls this process "reengineering," which breaks the perceived link between expenditure per student (or student-faculty ratio) and educational quality (p. 8). This link is one of those fundamental assumptions that the work on cost-efficiencies is designed to question and break apart. But to be able to break this long-time assumption and educate more students at a lower cost per student requires substituting capital for labor through the auspices of instructional design. Although this approach will most likely mean higher development costs, it can eventually be realized in lower delivery costs.

Substituting Capital for Capital

This substitution might correctly be a subset of the substitution of capital for labor, but given many institutions' interest in using online learning to use their existing buildings more efficiently, these studies are discussed separately. Examples of capital-for-capital substitutions can be found in studies from the University of Central Florida (UCF), the University of Virginia, and Vanderbilt University. By delivering portions of a course online, UCF saved classroom space: two or three sections could be scheduled in the same classroom, saving the cost of building new space or renting space. In Milam's description of costing decisions at the University of Virginia (2000), the cost of renting local commercial space ($25 per square foot per year) is incorporated. By recognizing a cost for space, Milam can conclude that online courses represent no space cost to the institution and traditional courses represent a space cost (with mixed-model courses carrying a moderate cost for space). Farmer (in Bodain and Robert, 2000) estimates that the absence of a physical building would save up to 15 percent of the cost of traditional courses. Vanderbilt used simulation software in sophomore-level electrical engineering and found that student learning in the simulated labs was as good as for students in the physical labs. Campbell and others (2004) conclude that simulation software could "replace some physical labs" (p. 9), which would also lower the ongoing cost of equipment and supplies for the physical labs.

This area clearly requires further study, especially in states expecting greater demand for access to higher education from growing numbers of high school graduates. Irrespective of the growing demand for access, states with constrained budgets might also wish to study these alternatives further.

Substituting Lower-Cost Labor for Higher-Cost Labor

Instructional design also allows for the substitution of lower-cost labor for the higher cost of faculty. It is not an argument for replacing full-time faculty with part-time instructors in the absence of redesigning the course. Redesign incorporates the expertise of full-time faculty where their expertise is essential to student learning such as where higher-order learning is the goal, learning problems must be diagnosed, or complex projects must be evaluated and appropriate feedback occur. So this is an argument for using faculty expertise differently and using lower-cost labor when a lower level of expertise seems appropriate.

Course redesign projects include several examples where online modules, virtual labs, computer-mediated exercises, online quizzes and tests, and grading help students learn more while using higher-cost faculty labor less. These options also are a way to use capital (the designed instruction embedded in online or Web-based settings) for labor, but when instructional support is still necessary, the design can be sufficiently robust so that instructional support can be provided by lower-cost assistants. In their place, the sample courses used graduate assistants, teaching assistants, undergraduate peers, and part-time instructional staff to answer technical questions, diagnose simple learning mistakes, and provide other assistance. Even lower-cost faculty (perhaps assistant professors) can lower the cost of a course if the original designer was a full professor. Rio Salado College used a course assistant to answer non-math-related questions, which accounted for 90 percent of the interactions with students (Twigg, 2002). Arvan and others (1998) describe a set of courses at the University of Illinois that used graduate assistants to teach and undergraduate peer-tutors and peer-to-peer interaction to answer basic questions.

The Seven Principles at Work

Chickering and Ehrmann (1996) have taken the seven principles for good practice in undergraduate education first described by Chickering and Gamson (1987) and applied them to online classes. Each of the seven principles can be achieved through online learning:

(1) encourage contact between students and faculty,
(2) develop reciprocity and cooperation among students,
(3) encourage active learning,
(4) give prompt feedback,

(5) emphasize time on task,

(6) communicate high expectations, and

(7) respect diverse talents and ways of learning.

These practices are intended to improve learning for students, but online learning can also achieve cost-efficiencies while promoting these practices. Let us examine each principle to see how it might be used to improve student learning and influence cost-efficiency. For example, contact between students and faculty need not always take the form of lecture-style classes, where the interaction is in fact quite minimal; a redesigned course might use one-on-one time with faculty for student questions of a more complex nature and use lower-cost instructional staff to provide greater contact of a more basic nature. Online discussion forums can minimize passive learning, as they help develop cooperation among students at the same time they can allow students to answer each others' questions (and thereby use less faculty time). Active learning through online simulations or course assignments increases student learning, which can in turn result in better completion rates and lower drop-failure-withdrawal (DFW) rates (so-called by Twigg, 2003a). Prompt feedback can be provided through online quizzes that explain why the response is incorrect and encourage mastery of course content. Time on task can be improved as the learning experience is more involving and motivating to students. High expectations can be conveyed through course design or messages and do not depend solely on faculty doing so in person. Last, as expertise is gained with instructional design and especially designing multiple pathways through the learning material, students may opt for a pathway that uses their talents best (or conversely, a talent they need to improve). In these examples, quality is improved and student learning improved, but cost-efficiencies can also occur.

Another question to ask is whether using professionals during the design of the course improves activities or practices normally associated with the seven principles. Brown, Myers, and Roy (2003) evaluated courses at Washington State University that used an instructional designer and those that did not. Results indicated that the course design process increased faculty-student interaction, student-student interaction, feedback, and time on task. The authors note that many faculty are not familiar with the seven principles and that by working with an instructional designer, they become not only more familiar with the principles but also more likely to integrate technology that uses the practices supported by the principles. A study by Henderson (2004), also done at Washington State University, found that courses that went through a quick course review by instructional design professionals did as well as those that went through a long formal design process. In other words, perhaps a more cursory review of online courses that uses the seven principles may be as effective as a more intensive development process. This finding argues for the importance of incorporating design principles in a short review process of online offerings and perhaps using the more intensive process for courses that require more bells and whistles or for faculty development when they are new to online courses.

The Benefits of Instructional Design

Using instructional design to make coursework wholly or even partially online has several benefits. Certainly studies have found that grades improve (Fisher and Nygren, 2000) on midterm exams, final exams, and other assessments of student knowledge of course content. At Pennsylvania State University, students in the redesigned courses had 68 percent correct answers (compared with 60 percent correct for students in traditionally taught courses); at Carnegie Mellon, students in a redesigned statistics course increased their performance by 22.8 percent; at Florida Gulf Coast University, average scores on a standardized test were 85 percent (compared with 70 percent for students in the traditional course); at the University of Iowa, students enrolled in a redesigned introductory chemistry course performed better on an American Chemical Society examination in two comparisons with students in the traditional course (65.4 to 58.4 and 61.0 to 52.4); at the University of Massachusetts–Amherst, examination questions in biology were redesigned so that 67 percent of the questions tested reasoning or problem-solving skills rather than only 23 percent of the questions in an earlier version of the test; at Drexel University and Carnegie Mellon, final examinations were made more difficult as a result of the additional student learning occurring as a result of course redesign (Twigg, 2005, 2003a). At Michigan State University, students in a redesigned introductory physics course had an 11 percent increase in performance, and 32 percent achieved grades higher than 3.5 (compared with 18 percent in the traditional course) (Fisher and Nygren, 2000). Arvan and others (1998) also found that the asynchronous learning network courses boosted students' examination performance and that students especially appreciated taking quizzes when it was convenient for them and retaking the quizzes so that they could learn from their mistakes.

But students also drop the course less often, fail at a lower rate, and withdraw less often. The University of Southern Maine lowered its DFW rate from 28 percent to 19 percent in the redesigned introductory psychology course. At the University of Idaho, the percentage of students earning a D or failing grade was cut by more than half. At Drexel University, the DFW rate for computer programming dropped from 49 percent to 38 percent; at Florida Gulf Coast, the rate dropped from 45 percent to 11 percent; at Indiana University–Purdue University Indianapolis, the rate dropped from 39 percent to 25 percent in introductory sociology; at the University of New Mexico, the rate dropped from 42 percent to 25 percent in introductory psychology; Rio Salado College increased completion rates from 59 percent to 64.8 percent (Twigg, 2003a, 2002). At Baruch College, a course in college literacy for students with poor reading and writing skills experienced a failure rate of almost 50 percent; when the course was redesigned to use real-time computer conferencing, 75 percent of the students passed the course (Ehrmann, 1999). Certainly students will benefit from these improvements as will institutions that can improve the cost per passing student in a constrained budget.

Thus, redesigned courses have "increased course-completion rates, improved retention, better student attitudes toward the subject matter, and increased student satisfaction with the new mode of instruction" (Twigg, 2003a, p. 24). Improved learning is the result of changing the pedagogy and educational philosophy so that the course stresses active, experiential learning. The passive learning created by a dependence on lecturing is replaced by active learning, including modules, tutorials, exercises, quizzes, and projects. Pennsylvania State University's redesign of elementary statistics, hands-on experience with data analysis and low-stakes "readiness assessment" testing involved students in their learning more directly and increased their motivation to learn (Harkness, Lane, and Harwood, 2003). In other words, active learning has its own rewards, and good instructional design simply uses the pedagogy to increase students' engagement and learning. "Students learn math by doing math, not by listening to somebody talk about doing math" (Twigg, 2003a, p. 25).

Twigg (1999, pp. 9–10) has also emphasized, however, that for course redesign to be effective, an institution must be ready and eight "course readiness criteria" must be met:

Improvements in the course potentially must have a high impact on the curriculum.

The course must offer the possibility of capital-for-labor substitution.

Decisions about curriculum in the department, program, or school must be made collectively (beyond individual faculty members).

Faculty must be able and willing to incorporate existing curricular materials into the project to focus work on redesign rather than on creating materials.

Project participants must have the requisite skills.

The course's expected learning outcomes and a system for measuring their achievement must be identified.

The faculty members involved must have a good understanding of learning theory or access to expert partners.

For the innovation to be self-sustaining in the future, institutions must have a business plan to support the ongoing operation of the redesigned course.

This list of criteria is not just a screening tool, but it gives an institution a sense of whether it can benefit from redesigning courses. The list might prevent the unready institution from undertaking a costly redesign that it cannot benefit from and cannot maintain. On the other hand, an institution that is ready to make this next step toward finding ways to be cost-efficient and improve student learning can be assured that its investment in time, money, and people can have the payoff it desires.

Certainly readiness can play a role in the extent to which the institution can integrate technology. Twigg (2003b) notes that the course redesign projects tended to group themselves into several models. The Supplemental Model maintains the basic structure of a course (including all class meetings) but supplements the course with technology-based activities. The Replacement Model reduces class meetings and replaces them with online, interactive learning. The Emporium Model eliminates class meetings and allows the students to learn when they want to learn by accessing online learning materials and on-site help; Virginia Tech's Math Emporium is the best example of this approach. The Fully Online Model puts all instruction and support online as Rio Salado College did with four precalculus mathematics courses that used Academic Systems mathematics software and a large bank of problems. The Buffet Model allows students to choose among a variety of paths through the material based on their individual learning styles, abilities, and tastes (Twigg, 2003b). What is especially helpful about these approaches is understanding that an institution can choose among them—or choose different approaches for different courses or disciplines—and still achieve cost savings and improved student learning. These models may also represent a staged approach to experimenting with instructional design—from Supplemental through Replacement to Fully Online—that an institution and its faculty can follow as they learn more about how to do a good job of redesigning courses for online applications. In others, these approaches are in themselves a Buffet Approach to course redesign.

Instructional design will have an important impact on both the effectiveness and cost-efficiency of online courses. But reaping these benefits requires an upfront investment in other staff such as instructional designers and Web specialists as well as cooperation with faculty, the willingness of students to learn in this fashion, and an infrastructure to support these efforts. Instructional design is one cell that interacts with many other cells in the framework, an interaction that depends on activities and decisions made in other cells and that in turn influences what happens elsewhere. Fortunately, however, studies focusing on instructional design can give the institution some solid guidance on how to achieve cost-efficiencies through its online learning programs.

Content Is a New Opportunity

Content may be a novel factor to some, one that in the past was contained in the expertise of faculty, course and program curricula, textbooks, and libraries. But with the advent of online education comes the introduction of content that is contained in a new form: the course created by another entity, curricula available online, the freestanding online module, a simulation, a learning object, and electronic journals, e-books, and other assorted Web-based materials.

Perhaps the best example of the course created by another body is the tele-course (popular among many community colleges) that is telecast on local television stations and augmented by faculty at the community college. Online versions of this option are the Web sites and courses developed by publishers to accompany popular textbooks that are also augmented or adjusted by a local faculty member. Although borrowing, leasing, or purchasing another institution's online course has happened infrequently in the past, it is increasing in popularity, especially for institutions entering the online education arena.

Course curricula are available online through numerous course Web sites that are not embedded in a course management system. Go to your favorite search engine and search for a course—say, business management or technical writing—and hundreds of courses can be viewed and good ideas borrowed. But perhaps the most influential free online curriculum project is the MIT OpenCourseWare project (http://www.ocw.mit.edu) from the Massachusetts Institute of Technology. Syllabi, course notes, lectures, and exercises are available for many courses and can be downloaded by other higher education faculty, K–12 teachers, and students interested in independent learning. What is most interesting about this initiative is that it is not tied to an effort to enroll students in credit courses or to reap tuition or other monetary gain from access to the materials. In an early evaluation report, MIT (2005) documented that the site has been visited by 2.3 million separate visitors in one year (from November 2003 through October 2004) and that these visitors came from North America (36 percent of visitors), eastern Asia and western Europe (16 percent each), Latin America and eastern Europe (11 percent each), and the Middle East, Africa, Pacific, Central Asia, and Caribbean. Self-learners accounted for 48 percent of visitors; 15 percent of the visitors were educators who have master's or doctoral degrees (81 percent) and teach engineering or science, and a third of these educators had already adopted materials from the site. Materials have been translated into Spanish, Portuguese, and Chinese, and the Open-CourseWare model is being adopted by universities in the United States,

China, Japan, Spain, France, and India. Although it is not clear at this stage to what extent this project will influence curricular sharing among higher education institutions in the United States, it is certainly an effort to watch with interest.

One area of enormous growth has been the development of online learning objects collected in learning object repositories that specialize in a particular content or level of application, or by the institutions that contributed them. Multimedia Educational Resources for Learning and Online Teaching (MERLOT) is a prime example of this approach, although many other repositories exist. MERLOT began as an effort of California State University system institutions to develop and then review learning objects in the sciences, but it rapidly grew to include other institutions from the United States and many more disciplines. (For a list of learning object repositories, go to http://www.elearning.utsa.edu/guides/LO-repositories.htm.) In fact, the list of more than twenty-five repositories holding hundreds of online exercises, java applets, simulations, and miniprograms to address learning in mathematics, science, the humanities, graphic design, and almost every other discipline is quite impressive. Even a cursory search of these repositories might make it clear how much time and effort it takes for a faculty person to locate, evaluate, accommodate, and use a learning object in a course, an effort of time that might pay off for student learning if an object exists and works well with the course and students enrolled. Here is the cost conundrum of learning objects: although the potential for cost savings exists, it requires an enormous expenditure of cost in terms of faculty time. So until there are easier ways to search and locate learning objects, the task for faculty to use them represents a cost to the institution that may, or may not, be acceptable.

Let us contrast the OpenCourseWare concept with the learning object initiative. Although both have value for improving student learning and addressing costs, they are different in important ways. Courseware appears in a form recognizable to student and faculty alike; materials have a context (a course name or title) that another faculty person can identify quickly, access, and peruse. It has a structure that is immediately understandable: objectives, activities, readings, and so on. Courseware can easily be found by entering a course name in a search engine, as many faculty have posted their course materials on the Web. On the other hand, learning objects are often in repositories that faculty must become aware of and find, search, and evaluate. Objects are often without context, and faculty must find a course or context for them. They also require faculty to plan for or design activities around their use. These differences may explain why the OpenCourseWare initiative has had a greater impact than learning objects, although one hopes the learning object initiative can soon overcome these current drawbacks.

Several writers have promoted the use of existing content to save monies for higher education. Jones and Matthews (2002) mention that one way to lower development costs is to "find ways to use content that has been developed elsewhere" (p. 5). Howell, Williams, and Lindsay (2003) mention that standardizing content through the reuse of learning objects is one of the thirty-two important trends that administrators must understand. Critical to the use of learning objects is the drive to individualize learning. For example, Frydenberg (2002) states that "the central issue in courseware development at the moment is the potential for developing reusable learning objects, tagging them in a systemic way, storing them in well-designed databases, and retrieving and recombining them with other objects to create customized learning experiences for specific needs" (p. 4). Despite a laudable focus on improving student learning, what may perhaps be read between the lines of these statements of support for reusing content is a lot of work on the part of faculty and other staff.

The issue of the cost-efficiencies of reusing or borrowing and revising existing content is a crucial one to resolve. The example of the Open University is one of developing excellent course materials and using them for many students and many offerings of the course. It is also used by the University of Phoenix, which has invested in the development of courses that are then used without modification by its instructors. Certainly electronic journals and e-books also add to cost-efficiency. Montgomery and King (2002) make the case that electronic journals—certainly a historic source of important content for courses— are more cost-effective per use when they are widely accepted and used. Looney and Sheehan (2001) describe some popular uses for e-books, which may include animations, video, Web links, or simulations and which can be updated from the publisher's Web site to include updated information or products. In this case, the cost of development is borne by the e-book publisher but upgrades to the existing e-book may still carry a fee, and it undoubtedly takes time on the part of faculty to be familiar with the elements of the e-book, which would change periodically and therefore add to the workload.

Lasseter and Rogers (2004) provide several lessons learned while implementing an online core curriculum using learning objects for the university system of Georgia. The lessons include the importance of creating development teams, quality instructional design, and faculty readiness to work with learning objects; such lessons are not new, but they stress again the importance of time when using learning objects. Mason, Pegler, and Weller (2005) describe and evaluate a master's level course entirely made from 155 learning objects; students seemed to use the objects to modify the course to address their needs and then the objects were reused in other courses or settings. When reused, the objects did need to be revised, but this use accounted for only "a fraction (estimated at less than 5%) of the time that it took to write the original learning objects" (p. 104). Again, use of these objects takes time, but they do seem to have pedagogical advantages.

Littlejohn (2003) stresses the reuse of online resources, providing a solid analysis of why they are currently not as widely used as one might like. Currently objects are used differently in different contexts that may require modification, learner support must be provided (not all objects work on students' computers), and the lack of standardization and interoperability all add to the cost of using learning objects. Efforts are under way, however, to help improve the likelihood of sharing objects through improving the granularization of objects (breaking them down into usable parts), developing tools to support sharing, and providing exemplary courses to give faculty ideas about how objects can be integrated into courses in ways that enhance student learning. What is exciting about such ongoing efforts is the promise that users will eventually find approaches that will be more cost-efficient than is currently the case.

So far, the emphasis has been on the added cost in terms of faculty time and the need for instructional designers or other staff to revise or create learning objects. These barriers are not the only ones to greater use of learning objects or using courses developed by someone else. The NIH syndrome ("not invented here") has kept some faculty from considering the use of content developed at another institution, but given the growing use of telecourses, learning object repositories, and students who take online courses for use in their on-campus program, perhaps this situation is changing (Harley, Maher, Henke, and Lawrence, 2003; Johnstone, 2002). In any case, institutions need answers for how to make sharing content work well for faculty, programs, and the institution's attempt to be more cost-efficient. At the present time, we simply do not have the answers.

Infrastructure Is Necessary

The focus of this section is the technical infrastructure needed for online learning and its role in achieving cost-efficiencies. It also addresses several administrative issues, including outsourcing or leasing infrastructure or technical support and centralization or decentralization of various services.

In a survey of 4,130 U.S. postsecondary institutions about their distance education activity in 2000–01, the National Center for Education Statistics (2003) asked what barriers kept institutions that did not intend to begin distance education from starting such efforts in the next three years. Twenty-four percent of these institutions mentioned "limited technological infrastructure to support distance education" (p. viii), compared with 39 percent of this same group of institutions for which technological infrastructure was "not at all" a factor.

What should one make of these figures? Perhaps the best explanation is simply that most institutions now possess the basic technological infrastructure to offer distance education (or online learning) because they have needed to upgrade their internal networks and access to external networks to support current instructional operations. Wiring, servers, routers, intranets, computers, and software packages are a necessary tool for the modern institution. Therefore, although adding more online learning programs may place extra demands on these systems or force the institution to upgrade or expand its infrastructure, these costs are perhaps necessary simply to support ongoing instructional uses of on-campus programs or the university's expanding list of online student services for on-campus students. In other words, the lack of infrastructure may be seen as a barrier to distance education but not to expanding other services. Simply put, the institution needs to invest in its infrastructure in any case, irrespective of online education, just to stay competitive with other institutions. In any case, although the demands placed on technical infrastructure will likely continue to grow on all institutions as a result of online learning, online student services, ERP systems, campus portals, online library resources, and research functions, online learning may be responsible for generating only a portion of this demand.

Some institutions, however, have not invested in their technical infrastructure to the same extent and are facing high-cost investments. For these institutions especially, Rumble's assertion (n.d.) that because "expenditures for technology require significant amounts of money, . . . investment appraisal" (p. 1) is necessary to help the institution define costs and benefits related to the technology investment as well as the "opportunity cost of capital" (p. 1). Although having the best and most up-to-date technical infrastructure may be necessary for many institutions, it may not be deemed necessary for all. In other words, there may be good reasons to forgo an investment in technical infrastructure: the money would be better spent elsewhere, or the amount of money required to be competitive is not available. For example, a survey by the National Center for Education Statistics (2003) found that 44 percent of institutions that do not expect to offer distance education in the next three years believed that distance education does not fit with the institutional mission; 33 percent of these institutions mentioned the high cost of program development, and 22 percent mentioned a lack of perceived need.

But let us return to the institutions that have chosen to make this investment and to keep their infrastructure current and sized to handle the growing demands placed on it. Costing additions to the infrastructure needed solely to address online learning certainly must be incorporated into analyses of cost-efficiencies. Pumerantz and Frances (2000) provide an extensive list of costs related to implementing a new technology, including the cost of the technology as well as the time and effort of personnel. These costs include revising the institution's strategic plan, reorganizing units, marketing the technology to faculty, securing funding, negotiating contracts, providing professional development, redesigning programs, providing student support services, revising human resources management, adapting the physical plant and equipment, updating property management systems and library operations, incorporating legal costs (such as intellectual property rights and copyrights), and managing change at all levels of the organization (pp. 243–246). In other words, adding a new technology incurs a variety of costs. The next task is to determine the proportion of these costs devoted to online learning and to add them to calculations of cost-efficiencies, if possible. Or simply consider the technical infrastructure a "shared commons" that is essential to all institutional activities. Unfortunately, as Green and Jenkins (1998) make clear, most institutions do not have a clear picture of how much the institution spends on technology, largely because this spending is decentralized and made by departments throughout the institution. Therefore, costing this enterprise or allocating appropriate costs to online learning is particularly difficult.

But if new or expanded infrastructure is needed to handle new or increased uses of online learning, what might these infrastructure costs be? Hislop (2001b) mentions such costs as communications (such as additional leased lines from the institution to the Internet or dial-up modems and student access to the Internet), the cost of adding more servers, and the cost of new technical staff to handle the increased workload. Depending on the status of its infrastructure, additional costs might include equipment, software, consultants, and maintaining and upgrading existing systems.

Does outsourcing help lower costs? Several institutions have attempted to lower costs or control their growth by outsourcing infrastructure or support. Leach and Smallen (1998, 2000) and the COSTS project have collected data from more than one hundred institutions and tested whether outsourcing decreased the unit cost of providing various services. Outsourcing desktop computer repair, for example, was found to be an economical strategy, especially for small institutions (those with fewer than three thousand full-time enrollments). Unfortunately, outsourcing has a downside. Bates (n.d.) has correctly identified that outsourcing also outsources the development of expertise; in other words, it forgoes an important opportunity for the institution's staff and faculty to learn the new skill being outsourced. If that skill is potentially valuable, and especially valuable to improving the institution's competitive advantage with regard to other institutions or valuable for improving student learning, why would an institution choose to outsource it?

Leasing is another tactic to lower or control costs and improve cost-efficiencies. This tactic has been most frequently applied to computers, which an institution could lease from a private provider rather than purchase. Doing so has the advantage of turning computers from a purchase that may take advantage of temporary "budget dust" to a long-term expense that can be included in the institution's annual budget and spread over several years (McCollum, 1999). Only 14 percent of institutions lease computers, however, largely because the price of computers has continued to drop, making their purchase more attractive. Seton Hall University, for example, leased a state-of-the-art central computer (Landry, 2000). Leasing shifted these technology expenditures from the capital budget to the operating budget and reduced the entry cost of implementing activities that required the central computer (p. 210).

The decision to lease equipment clearly depends on institutional preference, but it may also be influenced by the institution's size. Leach and Smallen (1998, 2000) found that the cost of providing desktop computer repair was less in larger institutions, where expertise was more likely to be available on campus. Small institutions can possibly achieve economies of scale by joining in consortia or partnership arrangements with other institutions. Another tactic that may be related to institutional size is the use of tech-savvy students to perform certain technical support tasks—computer repair or the helpdesk, for example—with an associated lowering of cost by using lower-cost labor.

Another organizational issue that seems to influence cost-efficiency is the decision to decentralize the provision of services. Bates (2000b) argues that decentralization is a "recipe for chaos, and it always results in massive duplication" (p. 185). Further, there is no center of expertise and no requirement for faculty to standardize approaches. Bates is not arguing for a totally centralized function but a "lightly coordinated decentralized model" (p. 185), one where a small central unit has specialized and skilled staff and decentralized units where faculty expertise can grow with their experience with online learning. Many universities have decentralized some elements of technical support but retained a centralized unit that can handle more detailed or complicated issues. Given the culture of higher education, perhaps the "lightly coordinated" set of organizational approaches is the only realistic choice.

Clearly the investment in infrastructure is a large cost and can affect the ability of online learning to achieve cost-efficiencies—especially if an institution's infrastructure is inadequate or many additions and upgrades are necessary to tackle the world of online education. Many institutions, however, probably have sufficient infrastructure to support online learning, because the same infrastructure is now necessary to provide so many other services to modern students with a taste for online, convenient services. Although online learning may be only one of these services, the demands it places on the technical infrastructure—the networks and the people who support them—are likely to grow as enrollments, courses, and programs go online and economies of scale make cost per use more reasonable.

Policies Are Needed

The seventh factor—the factor with the most issues and the least available research—comprises policies. Ten policy areas are included in this discussion: tuition, state subsidy, faculty, students, sharing content, time, vision, strategic planning, budgets, and class size. This list is a modification of the policy analysis framework proposed by King and others (2000), but some topics have been added that appear in the literature. The reader should note that only one policy area—policies that affect faculty work—has a body of research but that it does not address the issue of cost-efficiency. Therefore, this area is prone to speculation and requires thoughtful research.

Tuition and Fees

The first policy issue, tuition and fees, is important to discussions of cost-efficiency for several reasons. First, the level of tuition is certainly a cost to students, which is important if the analysis of cost-efficiency includes student costs. Second, it is critical to achieving the breakeven point or charging enough so that development and delivery costs can be recovered. Third, perhaps more important to institutions is the practice of charging in-state tuition for online courses, which forgoes dollars from out-of-state students.

In 1997–98, 74 percent of institutions charged the same tuition for distance education and on-campus courses as well as out-of-state students (National Center for Education Statistics, 1999); 57 percent of institutions charged comparable tuition and fees for distance education and on-campus courses (p. vi). Wentling and Park (2001) found that the University of Illinois charged all students the same, in-state rate. Fourth, Wentling and Park (2002) had to allow for tuition waivers to be used, which meant that more fee-paying students had to enroll to offset the loss of revenue caused by the tuition waivers. Fifth, the practice of using one tuition rate may argue for breaking down the distinction between types of students such as online versus on campus and resident versus nonresident. Or it may imply breaking down the distinction among program types or delivery modes such as face-to-face instruction versus online education. Some campuses have had to rethink their tuition and fee policy for online courses when online students object to paying fees for services they will never use (such as fees for building construction, health and wellness centers, and activities on campus). In any case, one advantage of understanding the different costs of online coursework is to rationalize the tuition and fee policy, as online students may not use some on-campus resources but may use online services, especially student services and library support, to a greater extent than on-campus students.

Tuition policy does incorporate a great many concerns. The practice of charging lower tuition to students in online courses is rooted in a set of values that stress improving access to higher education as well as making college affordable—laudable public policy goals. This pricing practice should increase the lower-cost institution's market share among students sensitive to price or help an institution enter a new market successfully. On the other hand, waiving tuition (or the portion of tuition assessed to out-of-state students) is lost revenue that might have helped the institution recover the costs of developing online courses. The strategy of keeping tuition lower is in direct opposition to the practices of higher-price institutions that charge higher tuition to take advantage of students ready, willing, and able to pay such prices (or have employers willing to do so). Miller (2001) calls this practice value-priced tuition or the "value of the program in a market place" (p. 166), which recognizes the willingness of some students to pay a premium price for a program that represents value to them.

This situation allows institutions to charge a premium price for programs such as the M.B.A. but then use some of these funds to support other activities that have value to the institution and students.

One hopes that the decision of how to price an online course or program and whether it is higher or lower than other offerings is subjected to as much scrutiny as other assessments of cost-efficiency. Certainly tuition policies affect how cost-efficient an online program can be. The majority of tuition decisions, however, are made for reasons that do not relate to whether an online program can become cost-efficient or when it might do so. Although tuition should not be set solely to achieve the crossover point discussed earlier, it is clearly an important public policy that is a tool for achieving a range of other public ends such as increasing access and keeping college affordable. The decision of how to set tuition or the online program's price is relevant to the issue of online learning's cost-efficiency, yet it is often set without attention to achieving that end. In other words, tuition, although critical to any analysis of cost-efficiency, is a policy that carries a number of policy ends that may contradict or simply be irrelevant to cost-efficiency. This point is important in any future discussions of whether online learning is or can be cost-efficient.

State Subsidies

A second policy issue for public institutions is the effect of state subsidies. Smith (2000) has noted that state subsidies are a competitive advantage for public institutions, which can mask unprofitable online courses or programs. An institution that receives a subsidy cannot be said to operate as a "real business," because it is leveraging distance education initiatives against its existing resources (faculty, staff, libraries, campus networks) (Green, 1997). Although it may be true, one can reason that unprofitable online programs can and do serve worthy public objectives by providing a lower-cost or accessible education for the state's residents. Such a public policy goal might continue to be worthy of state support. State subsidies for higher education institutions also recognize that following requirements for strict profitability (that is, producing greater revenue than it costs to provide the education) in any and all educational programs may not be advisable for the state. States benefit from so-called unprofitable activities as institutions struggle to implement online learning and thereby learn how to improve student learning in all programs. States benefit from unprofitable programs that produce trained graduates in fields no individual citizen could afford to pay for on his or her own. States benefit when unprofitable activities produce research, advances in practice, and business spin-offs that shore up their economy. These arguments depend on public policy strategies and values, not research relating to cost-efficiency. In fact, research-based answers may be long in coming, because questions about the role of subsidies have not been a focus of higher education researchers.

Faculty Work

The third policy area incorporates the range of policies that shape faculty work: workload, professional development, remuneration and reward, promotion and tenure, intellectual property, and the unbundling of the faculty role. Developing online courses demands an enormous commitment of time from faculty, both to learn the new skills and to develop the course (either alone or with a team) so that it works in this format. Morgan (2000) found that faculty reported a 52.5 percent increase in time spent to develop and teach online courses, a similar finding to the NEA (2000), Eggins (2000), and Boettcher (2004), among others. And although a design team may produce a better online course, a team may require a larger time expenditure on the part of faculty to collaborate and discuss alternatives with team members. In any case, delivering an online course may also require more time from faculty, especially if it has not been redesigned to replace faculty labor with online modules or lower-cost labor. In the absence of course redesign, it is also important to consider time-saving policies (not answering every e-mail, declaring a personal "day off" from e-mail, or forming student groups to answer immediate questions) to help faculty manage the increased workload of the class. In each case, the institution may need to evaluate its workload policies for faculty. One option has been to temporarily reduce workload when faculty are developing a class or granting a one-term course release when they are in the steepest part of the learning curve. This policy may have limited usefulness, however, as it may not be practical to grant so much faculty release time.

State and institutional policies that require faculty to teach a set credit load may ultimately prove to be a brake to developing online instruction. Faculty time needs to be used differently from the way it was in the past, requiring a heavier investment of time in development and learning new processes. Therefore, credit-based workload "policies and procedures that don't recognize this reality often get in the way of innovation" (Jones and Matthews, 2002, p. 8).

Another workload policy is whether teaching online will be considered "in load" or "out of load." The latter assumes the course or some other source of funding exists to pay the faculty person to teach the course. An important message is hidden in the policy that teaching online will be "in load," however; it implies that teaching online is a standard activity of the institution and that it is within the faculty's regular work obligations. This area is also ripe for data on what institutions are doing and whether or not these policies work well.

To be successful, online learning requires that faculty learn new skills; therefore, policies on professional development for faculty are important. Will it be funded by the institution? Will faculty be remunerated for their participation? Such policies send different messages to faculty: the institution values professional development and recognizes that it requires a commitment of time and effort above and beyond current duties. On the other hand, these policies are difficult to sustain as more faculty become involved with online learning and call on the institution's professional development resources. Fortunately, the research on faculty motivation characterizes faculty as less motivated by external incentives such as money than others might expect. Schifter (2000, 2002) surveyed faculty and administrators and found that faculty who taught online were motivated by intrinsic factors, while administrators thought faculty participated as a result of extrinsic motivators. Fredericksen and others (2000) found similar results; faculty were motivated to teach online because of an interest in the Internet, online teaching, or student learning. Betts (1998) had similar results: faculty were motivated by intrinsic factors such as intellectual challenge, and extrinsic factors such as credit toward promotion or merit pay did not affect their involvement. Rockwell, Schauer, Fritz, and Marx (1999) found that 83 percent of faculty surveyed thought that providing innovative instruction was the largest incentive to teach online.

These studies paint a consistent and much different picture of faculty from that administrators, legislators, and external critics paint. Many faculty want to move into online education because it represents the future of higher education and they are committed to helping students learn. Other faculty seem to be strongly motivated by achieving student learning; Hartman, Dziuban, and Moskal (2000) found that faculty with experience teaching in asynchronous learning networks were satisfied with the increased flexibility and interaction with students. In other words, they argue, "faculty satisfaction and student outcomes are strongly related" (p. 155), which implies that student success is not only motivating for faculty but also is the reason for their involvement in online education. In fact, for those faculty who are "entrepreneurs" (Hagner and Schneebeck, 2001) or "innovators," "early adopters," or "early majority" (Rogers, 1995), perhaps it is the "policy-free" environment that allows faculty to freely experiment (Meyer, 2002a). In other words, the lack of institutional policies regulating faculty or online education is a boon to faculty wanting to experiment, innovate, and explore new options. This argument might be a good one for leaving the policy environment as it is (unless a policy is acting as a barrier) and leaving professional development up to the individual motivations of faculty.

One of the early policies to gain faculty support for distance or online education was to pay faculty to develop the course or to deliver it (essentially the same as paying them to teach the course "out of load"). Goldberg and Seldin (2000) stress that in preparing an online course, two arguments underscore the importance of paying faculty above their base pay: the importance of getting the course ready quickly, which may require an intense effort that is above the norm, and the need for the institution to own the online course, which requires compensation for faculty. This practice of paying faculty for developing courses has waned of late, partly because of constrained budgets but also because of the growth in online courses. When an activity is new, providing incentives to encourage involvement appears to be a sound policy. But as the activity grows, it becomes less practical to maintain. Institutions beginning an online effort might do well to evaluate whether pursuing a policy of incentives is a good idea, whether it can be maintained, or whether the culture of faculty at the institution will mean the activity is dropped if the policy cannot be maintained.

Perhaps the policies mentioned most frequently in the literature are promotion and tenure. These policies must recognize that developing and delivering online courses are legitimate instructional efforts and important contributions to a program or department (Goldberg and Seldin, 2000). It is not an argument for eliminating or diminishing a requirement for research but perhaps for strengthening and recasting the requirements for teaching to include online coursework. Junior faculty need to know that their involvement in online education will not be counted against them but will be recognized as an innovation that has value for their professional development and for the institution's reputation. It requires not only a review and revision of these policies—time consuming in themselves—but also an extensive educational program for all faculty so that they understand the new standards and do not inadvertently continue to apply the old standards. We simply do not know whether changing these policies will affect faculty involvement in online learning, although it is reasonable to assume so.

A policy that has gained a lot of attention from faculty groups is the institution's intellectual property policy. Institutional ownership of online courses has been claimed as a result of the institution's investment of resources in their development. Ownership is deemed essential if the upfront costs of development are to be recouped through multiple uses or multiple offerings. Later versions of intellectual property policies stress sharing: the faculty person owns the materials developed, but the institution is granted a no-cost license to use the materials. Other versions amenable to both parties are possible. Perhaps if these courses could be sold or leased or marketed to other institutions, one could see that intellectual property—as contained in an online course—might have market value. But so far it has not occurred, which may be because of the lack of a policy encouraging sharing of content or curricula among institutions. The uproar over intellectual property of online courses is the result of either a misperception of the marketable value of online courses or a rather more philosophical disagreement about employer-employee relations. Rather than an argument about losing control over the product of one's mind, intellectual property policy tends to clarify and magnify the disproportional power relationships between institutional managers and faculty. Faculty, who have traditionally felt in control of their professional lives, are reminded by the intellectual property policy that they are merely employees whose products are owned by another. Unfortunately, we do not know whether different intellectual property policies have different effects on the proliferation of innovative online education. Does institutional ownership of online courses dampen innovation, or does shared ownership encourage it? We do not know the answer.

A last policy issue that may affect faculty is the promotion of "unbundling" the faculty role. Although the traditional role of faculty includes course design, delivery, student assessment, and evaluation, unbundling separates these functions into different personnel: designers, assessment experts, and professional evaluators. The Open University, the University of Phoenix, and community colleges using prepackaged courses have effectively used this model. But it has not made inroads into traditional institutions, and the majority of faculty in U.S. institutions have not been affected by this trend. The issues are to what extent it will become a popular means of producing more cost-efficient instruction and whether it will be used in more limited situations or by individual institutions.

Students

The fourth policy area includes policies that affect students, including state policies that push students to graduate in fewer years, thereby using state and institutional resources more efficiently and opening up an enrollment slot for another student. Arnone (2004b) describes programs in place or proposed, including a program in Texas that pays off college loans for students who graduate promptly and a program at the University of Florida that guarantees a slot in any course required for the major. Florida was also considering a proposal that students taking more than the minimum number of credits to graduate would pay out-of-state tuition, the California State University system was considering applying higher fees for students who stay longer than desired and requiring students to finish general education courses for 60 credits, and the state colleges in Pennsylvania were considering using tuition policy to discourage students from enrolling in more courses than they intend to take and then dropping the least attractive one later, thus keeping other students out of the course. Another policy that affects students is granting priority to off-campus students for enrolling in online courses, in effect forcing on-campus students to take on-campus courses, a policy that students have challenged. It is not clear whether and to what extent such policies—geared toward improving students' efficient use of state resources—are effective in shaping or changing students' behavior or whether policies oriented toward punishing some behaviors (or placing a higher cost on them) are more or less effective than incentive policies. Last, it is unclear what the impact of such policies might be to the cost-efficiency of online learning.

Other policies that affect students and may also have an impact on the efficiency of online learning are any restrictions placed on withdrawing from courses (either in the number or timing of withdrawals), removals of incomplete or failing grades (again, either in limiting the number or timing of removing these grades), the number of times a student can retake a class, taking required courses out of sequence, and probably other policies that directly or indirectly affect students' efficient use of resources such as when and how often courses are offered and whether they are offered online. Moreover, policies that require students to own a computer—even though computers are now nearly ubiquitous among college freshmen—and requirements from accreditors or Congress that students' identity be authenticated when they are learning online or taking tests at a distance would add to the calculation of cost-efficiency for students.

Sharing Content

The fifth policy area is an emerging area of interest: the crafting of policy to encourage and support the sharing of content. Such a policy might include ways to share courses developed by other institutions, publishers, or other entities, and it might recognize that such a decision to share has saved the institution development costs or reduced the costs spent on development (already created content must still be adjusted for the current situation). It might provide benefits for programs using existing content, perhaps a greater share of the tuition returned to the department or greater access to resources on campus (such as instructional design staff) that will help in the transfer of existing content. In any case, much work will need to be done to develop and then evaluate such a policy over time.

Time Issues

The sixth policy area relates to a range of policies that deal with time: seat time, class meeting times, the academic calendar, and office hours. These policies resulted historically from the need to synchronize the implementation of education, which has not entirely receded from importance. For example, the pressure to coordinate academic calendars among campuses in a system is not merely bureaucratic but the result of a policy to encourage students to take advantage of courses offered by multiple institutions (especially online courses). But one of the truisms about the impact of the Internet has been the growing expectation that knowledge can be available twenty-four hours a day, seven days a week. Students demand more flexibility in their education, not simply because they have jobs, families, and other obligations but also because it is now possible to do so, courtesy of the Internet. E-mail and online courses make the faculty person seemingly available constantly, too, adding to faculty workload while improving responsiveness to students (who often expect immediate feedback to their e-mails).

Open enrollment and self-paced learning programs, however, present a small but growing pressure to change the current policy on having set academic calendars. Open enrollment programs, where students enroll whenever they desire rather than at a set time in the year, are growing in number. Self-paced learning, which is not tied to the quarter or semester of the offering institution, also questions the need for academic calendars and their strict beginning and ending dates. It is not clear at this juncture how big or influential these programs are and whether academic calendars will some day be a thing of the past. Such a change will not happen soon, simply because of the organizational advantages for students and institutions of start and end dates and because many institutions with the new flexible programs have found ways to operate within the strictures of the current academic calendar.

Seat time is another policy that has taken a beating in recent years. Critics of higher education argue that the policy of enforcing seat time requirements keeps higher education focused on input measures of teaching. Assessment advocates and accrediting associations argue that the focus of our efforts should be on student learning rather than on time spent in the classroom (Noone and Swenson, 2001). Adult students argue that seat time requirements treat them like children. State legislatures argue that the focus on seat time has kept higher education from experimenting with new learning models. Policies that enforce seat time requirements are manacles of the past.

If online learning has meant anything, it has meant that classes need not always be conducted synchronously. Although many classes still require some meetings for activities that can only or best be done face to face, set class meeting times are no longer always necessary. It does not imply that students do not invest time in their learning, only that learning need not be required to occur every Monday, Wednesday, and Friday at 10 A.M. in Main Hall. But if policies that require class schedules, classroom scheduling, or calculations of faculty workload or department productivity depend on the old model of synchronous classes, they may play havoc with the move to online education and play worse havoc for the attempt to accurately capture workload or productivity.

Policies requiring office hours make little sense in the online world. This policy is another vestige of a world where face-to-face interactions were the only ones possible and inspection of occupied offices was the only way to ensure faculty worked. It will be interesting to see whether the concept of "office hours" survives the online world of e-mail and whether online communications replace, augment, or confirm the need for old-fashioned office hours.

The Institution's Vision

The seventh policy area is the institution's vision for online learning, whether for off-campus or on-campus students. Bates (2000a, 2000b) stresses the importance of having a vision for teaching and learning and defining where technology or online learning fits in this vision (p. 43). This vision is not static, but one that creates the impetus for a journey that will be as important to the organization as the goal (Senge, 1990). "Visioning" helps those working in an organization to understand the "range of possibilities for teaching and learning that technology can facilitate and the possible outcomes, acceptable or otherwise, that might result" (Bates, 2000b, p. 45). It stresses teaching and learning and fitting technology within that vision. Technology does not drive the vision; it enables a future of teaching and learning that is sufficiently attractive to motivate the work of faculty and staff throughout the institution. As such, it is not a simple goal but a potential future that changes current behavior.

The type of vision statements that Bates (2000b) finds valuable are concrete and detailed and might address different scenarios for different learners. They might mix teaching models (from entirely face to face to entirely online), address the needs of such constituencies as adult workers, identify modules that can be reused in different settings, and address student service issues such as flexible admissions and enrollment (pp. 51–52). In fact, vision statements might be developed for the institution or departments, perhaps even for programs, as faculty and staff attempt to put form and function on their view of the future. This might also be the appropriate place for the institution and faculty to discuss and vision an educational philosophy that places a greater emphasis on constructivism or relying on pedagogies that encourage students to actively construct knowledge. Such a vision might affect both cost-efficiencies (because it requires additional faculty time and staff) and student learning (because constructivist learning has been tied to better learning and improved retention of learning).

Strategic Planning Process

The eighth policy area is the institution's strategic planning process, which provides the institution with a framework for decision making (Bates, 1995). Unfortunately, as recently as 1998 only 57 percent of public universities had a plan for distance education and 75 percent had a strategic plan for technology (Green, 1998). Because we do not know the content of these plans, it is unclear whether and to what extent planning has occurred for online learning initiatives. Important elements of a framework for decision making would help the institution make decisions on a strategic or institutional level and a tactical or instructional level, give equal attention to instructional and operational issues, identify important differences between technologies so that the appropriate mix can be chosen, and accommodate new technologies or developments in instruction (Eggins, 2000, p. 64). Waddoups, Hatch, and Butterworth (2003) make the same point, only stronger: "cost-effective redesign calls for a systemic plan to use online teaching and learning to provide higher quality and more efficient learning" (p. 103). In other words, planning is required, not an option. The Educause Learning Initiative has focused on designing learning spaces to support a number of learning experiences and objectives, both of which depend on having a vision for new learning environments but also a commitment to plan so appropriate resources can be made available and new environments can become a reality.

An important element of the planning process is the ability to identify trends that affect the institution. Bartolic-Zlomislic and Bates (1999) stress the importance of identifying those trendsetters—students, faculty, or staff— who identify problems and help the institution develop solutions. In other words, the first student wanting to enroll in courses online and the first faculty person wanting to access the library from home were the sort of trendsetters who helped institutions develop the new online services that are now the norm. Being aware of these individuals and paying attention to their input is critical to staying ahead of the curve.

Goldberg and Seldin (2000), Jones and Matthews (2002), and Dolence and Norris (1995) stress the use of planning to develop strategies that identify opportunities and provide solutions that benefit the institution. Goldberg and Seldin (2000) focus on the planning that provides detailed answers to questions of what will be offered online, to whom, with what features, and at what price—presuming a level of academic and financial planning that may not be the norm for many institutions at present. Jones and Matthews (2002) take a similar approach based on defining expectations regarding who should be served by online learning and how it will occur. Although they address state expectations for online learning, the point applies as well to institutions. Dolence and Norris (1995) take a different route, proposing the use of "expeditionary" initiatives that an institution launches to experiment with different solutions to learn what it can and test ideas in a real-world application. This sense of experimentation may actually capture most institutional approaches to planning at present. Keehn and Norris (2003) take this planning process a step farther and emphasize the cultivation of innovation and value oriented toward building a learner-centric focus and improved value for students and others. What is intriguing about this approach is its future orientation and stimulating rhetoric, which generates a more positive frame of mind than using planning to make decisions that are always rational, pecuniary, and thoroughly determined.

An emphasis on strategic planning may argue for a change in organizational structure in response to changes identified by the plan. Nygren and Fisher (1999) argue that various models of organizational change may be less important than the evolution of online learning. The tools used for instruction drive instructional practices, not the other way around. In this view, a strategic plan does not drive change; online learning drives change through the organization. This statement is intriguing, as it questions the ability of strategic planning to drive or even steer change. In any case, the need is certainly present for research on the competing roles of online learning and deliberate strategic planning to shape the institutions of the future.

Not much research has been done that incorporates a look at whether an institution's vision or strategic plan affected its success with online learning. Meyer (2002a) found that whether distance education appeared in the institution's mission statement or whether the state had a plan for distance education did not seem to affect the enrollment growth experienced by the five institutions included in the study. In other words, the market, as captured by the growing demand for distance education from students, seemed to be impervious to these planning issues, whether at the institutional or state level. We do not, however, have studies that ask whether having a vision or strategic plan allows institutions to do a better job with online learning or whether online learning is more cost-efficient in these institutions.

Budgeting

The ninth policy area is related to budgeting decisions and making them more rational and conscious, more regularized and recognized. Wentling and Park (2001) describe a policy at the University of Illinois that online programs be required to submit a business plan that projects the financial viability of the project. Boettcher (2004) and Green (1997) also argue for the development of business plans for distance learning programs. While an institution may not want to imply that decisions to proceed with all online programs should be based on a business plan that estimates profits, the implication that every program needs to understand its costs and potential revenues seems sound. Finkelstein and Scholz (2000) argue that funding for information technology needs to move from "year-end budget leftovers" to an operating expense (p. 14) included in annual budgets and treated as a recurring expense. Perhaps the same philosophy might be useful for online learning as well.

Class Size

The tenth policy area is class size, which affects students and budgets but is also related to so much else. Bishop (2002) discusses a decision to make the ideal class size no larger than twenty-five students, allowing the program discussed to recoup costs and still be pedagogically sound. Unfortunately, no "firm formula [exists] for determining the optimum number of students for e-learning programs" (Wentling and Park, 2002, p. 3). The optimal class size for online classes is a policy that affects cost-efficiency as surely as it affects so many other parts of the institution: the number of students served, faculty workload, the number of faculty required to address student demand, the capacity of or drain on institutional resources (secretaries, infrastructure, library support, for example), and how many times the course must be offered to achieve cost-efficiencies. The best argument for setting class size is one of instructional philosophy: limiting enrollments to ensure students have sufficient interaction with faculty and other students so that learning is ensured. Bates (2000b) argues that the appropriate number of students should be determined by educational philosophy, course design, and the number of students that can be handled by the technology. Yet perhaps the most common rationale for having a policy on class size is to assuage faculty concerns about online learning, to duplicate other policies affecting on-campus course enrollments, or to address legitimate faculty concerns about an expanding workload in the absence of a redesigned course. In any case, although research on class size for online courses is needed, it must recognize that instructional design affects the number of students that can be enrolled effectively (at no diminishment in student learning). An absolute policy on class size that does not recognize the impact of design would be counterproductive to achieving cost-efficiencies but might also be unnecessary, as it would limit the influence of further innovations that might improve learning irrespective of class size.

Looking Ahead

The next chapter focuses on some possible conclusions that can be drawn from this review of how factors in the framework are related to improving cost-efficiencies, answering some important questions from institutions and states about readiness and how to improve cost-efficiencies.

What Does It Mean for Institutions and States?

THIS CHAPTER ANSWERS THREE BROAD QUESTIONS using the research and literature cited in the preceding two chapters: (1) What questions should an institution or state ask itself before engaging in the pursuit of cost-efficiencies through online learning? (2) If the answers are yes to these questions, when and where will it be possible for an institution to achieve cost-efficiencies through online learning? (3) If the answer is yes, when and how can a state support an institution pursuing this path?

Are the Institution and the State Ready?

The first question to ask is whether the institution and state are ready to pursue seriously cost-efficiencies through online learning. One might assume that if they are considering cost-efficiency, they are already experienced with online learning, but that may not be the case. It might be logical to expect first some experience with exploring, doing, and adjusting online learning to the campus or state, but no evidence exists yet that this is a required step in the movement toward achieving cost-efficiencies.

Twigg's "readiness criteria" (1999) for institutions contemplating online learning and Bates's assertion (2000b) that a vision for online learning and strategic planning to make it a reality are important are logically appealing. These readiness factors reappear in the concluding chapter, where the topic is identifying the research we need to answer our questions. But the literature can tell us some things about what institutions and states will need to know and do to undertake this effort.

First, institutions need to have resources—specific resources at that. Certainly they need a technical infrastructure to support online education. Next, they need "other staff," including Web staff and instructional designers (among many others) who bring the expertise needed so that redesigning or putting courses online is possible. They need people who are skilled and familiar with the processes of substituting capital for labor and lower-cost labor for higher-cost labor, scaling courses so that learning improves and cost per student remains level or lowers, and choosing appropriate media for the learning task. Faculty need to learn new skills to contribute to the design process or to redesign their own courses without much help from other staff. All these efforts require resources. Put another way, the cost of developing cost-efficient online learning is much higher than that of other forms of education, but the higher development costs are essential if the institution has any chance of realizing lower delivery or administrative costs.

Second, institutions also need to assess attitudes on campus: are faculty open (if not eager) to tackle this new form of learning? Are students ready to learn this way? The research is fairly clear that attitudes can hamper the move to online learning, but ample evidence also exists that many faculty are motivated to do so and many students are eager to enroll. Other essential skills or attitudes are the capability and willingness to study the cost of what the institution is doing, not just in online learning, but in all facets of the operation. It is not an argument for one costing method over another, only that the institution selects one and uses it consistently. Without understanding costs, without a culture of evidence, knowing what is cost-efficient or whether cost-efficiency has been achieved is guesswork.

Third, this process takes time and certainly affects resources, because it will take more people more time to, say, redesign a course. Because innovations need to be integrated (Fahy, 1998), it takes time to assess the innovation, experiment with it, test its application, and find more and more applications throughout the organization, challenge the existing policies and structures, and change policies or practices that will support the innovation—the "glacial change" for which higher education is famous.

At this point, we should ask whether the state is ready to support the change. Does the state understand the amount of time it will take for this transformation? Can it give institutions the time they need to pursue this approach? Perhaps the pressures of a declining budget will force some states to pursue another approach, or perhaps the pressure is less immediate and time is available to design cost-efficiencies into online learning.

Perhaps more important than time is whether the state realizes that this transformation will take more resources for a period of time (perhaps a long period of time). Resources are needed to hire new staff with new and marketable skills commanding higher wages, to upgrade the infrastructure and various systems, to provide faculty with professional development to change their own courses, and more. If the budget situation is so dire that these resources cannot come from the state, then the state must be willing to allow institutions to reallocate resources from other functions and perhaps halt a different activity. A related issue is how the state will use incentives to encourage these changes and whether it will allow institutions to retain any costs saved as a result of online learning. A policy that allows institutions to retain cost savings is a powerful incentive and recognizes that resources can be generated to fuel new innovations or new online programs.

Neither caution to a state—that changing to online learning will take time and resources—negates its role in applying pressure for change. They do argue for caution and understanding that institutions are tackling a new way of educating students that is like "moving a battleship with your bare hands" (Weinstein, 1993, p. 1). Some tolerance for the messy, slow, and incremental nature of the process would be appreciated.

One caution is in order for both states and institutions to discuss and understand before determining whether they are ready to proceed. The economics of online courses are complex, fascinating, and not transparent. Under the right conditions, online learning can be cost-effective, but it can also bring in net profits for an educational institution. There is no easy money in this business, however. "It has to be earned." (Bartolic-Zlomislic and Bates, 1999, p. 16). Thus, failure may be just as likely if online learning is undertaken in a lackadaisical fashion or the institution chases facile profits with an unclear idea of what is really involved. States and institutions need to be ready for a complicated and challenging task, one that will be very different from others they have mastered in the past.

What Should Institutions Do?

If an institution is ready to proceed, when and where will it be possible for it to achieve cost-efficiencies through online learning? Fortunately, Twigg (2003a, 2003b) and others supply some clear answers.

First, identify the courses that enroll the most students and where enrollment is stable; they will be entry-level courses, perhaps most of them at the 100 or 200 level, courses needed by high-enrollment majors at the undergraduate or graduate level, courses that are particularly problematic or necessary to several majors, or courses that through multiple repetitions over the years enroll a lot of students. In other words, identify areas of the curriculum that can achieve economies of scale. Other targets for course redesign are courses that are particularly problematic for student learning, perhaps in mathematics or other areas. In this instance, however, the purpose will probably not be achieving economies of scale but improved learning for students—still a laudable goal worth pursuing.

Second, focus as much as possible on programs of study, whether degree programs or certificate programs, where enrollments are likely to be strong and stable. Check to see what the online competition is and how many competitors the program will face. Make sure the institution is ready, faculty, support staff, library services, and student services.

Third, hire and support a capable design staff. If you do not have this expertise on staff, find it. Make sure the people you hire are experts at instructional design and online learning, they can make wise decisions in the selection of appropriate media, they can improve student learning, and they understand how to achieve the substitutions of capital for labor, lower-cost labor for higher-cost labor, and capital for capital.

Fourth, put the design (or redesign) team together with faculty, instructional designers, Web support staff, and experts on your course management system. They need to look for ways to make these substitutions and improve student learning.

Fifth, provide faculty with help to learn these new skills and find ways to transmit these new skills to others in the institution. Evidence suggests that even modest training of faculty helps them improve both the quality and efficiency of online courses (Henderson, 2004); perhaps faculty are the best avenue for transferring some of these lessons about efficiency to lower-enrollment undergraduate courses or graduate programs. Professional development and improving the institution's learning curve are both necessary. In fact, investing in the learning curve (through professional development, design teams, and opportunities to share what others are doing and learning) is perhaps the only way the expertise of a small staff of designers or online learning experts can be transferred across an institution and its faculty.

Sixth, choose a costing method that works for the institution and stick with it. Results will be comparable not only among various efforts at the institution but also with studies from other institutions that use the same costing method. Ten valuable benchmarks will be available to all other institutions that are considering this change.

Seventh, calculate (and recalculate for different courses and situations) the crossover point. Understand the relationship between instructional decisions and economies of scale.

Eighth, track student behaviors (like dropping out or having trouble with independent learning), and study your choices, the cost of media, the impact of policies, changes made to faculty, and whether cost-efficiencies can be maintained. They are essential for improving the institution's practice but also for helping other institutions make informed decisions.

Ninth, help faculty understand the nature of these changes—that they will gradually modify their role and how they teach in many instances—but their involvement is necessary to make sure these changes improve student learning. Faculty are a valuable resource throughout these changes, and they need to be treated with respect and honesty. And faculty need to realize that change is coming and prepare for it.

What Should States Do?

If a state is ready to push for greater cost-efficiencies through online learning, what should it do?

First, understand the process. Cost-efficiencies do not happen as a result of wanting, asserting, or claiming them; they are the result of careful study, experimentation, revision, and constant innovation. Experimentation means occasional failures, which are as educational (perhaps more so) than many successes.

Second, give it time. Learning new ways of educating students takes time. Faculty and staff are busy with existing students and classes, obligations for service and research, and families; they are willing, for the most part, but they need to fit this learning into existing obligations.

Third, supply resources if at all possible, but if not, be willing to support reallocation of resources away from other activities. If you can provide them, additional resources during the development phase are especially important. "Good content development . . . is inevitably expensive" (Jones and Matthews, 2002, p. 7).

Fourth, realize that the major costs of online learning will continue to be "people costs—not the costs of technology" (Jones and Matthews, 2002, p. 8). This fact does not minimize the cost of the infrastructure, only that running the infrastructure and providing the services, training, and design are essentially people costs that will not decline.

This chapter has focused on summarizing advice to institutions, faculty, and states that can be derived from the two previous chapters, which reviewed the research on the elements and factors that help us understand how to achieve cost-efficiencies in online learning. The final chapter reviews the answers to the question about how to achieve cost-efficiencies, identifies the holes in our review of the research literature, and asks what research is needed.

What Do We Know? What Research Is Needed?

T HIS SECTION SUMMARIZES THE MAJOR FINDINGS from the research reviewed earlier. This will help us identify the "holes" in our understanding where more research is needed.

What We Know Today

Earlier chapters presented the research that documented how online learning can produce cost-efficiencies and cost-effectiveness. Online learning can improve student learning and reduce costs but only under several conditions and through various techniques.

The Conditions

Several conditions appear to have the largest impact on achieving cost-efficiencies and improved student learning. The institution must be serious about doing online learning well and efficiently, willing to invest in it to make sure students benefit and resources are used wisely, and able to track costs over time. The institution needs to assess its technical infrastructure and instructional design resources and make sure they are adequate to the task ahead. Courses or programs with large, stable enrollments where economies of scale are possible are a prime target for rethinking how a course may be made more efficient and better at producing student learning. For other courses and programs with smaller but consistent enrollments over time, faculty need to understand how to improve learning and achieve cost-efficiencies through instructional design and online learning principles.

The Techniques

Chief among the techniques for achieving cost-efficiencies is a careful redesign of courses that depend on instructional design and online applications of the seven principles (Chickering and Gamson, 1987). By first designing or redesigning the online course using principles known to improve student learning, faculty and institutions can be assured that they are serving students well. By then exploring the three substitutions (capital for labor, lower-cost labor for higher-cost labor, and capital for capital), institutions can find ways to use faculty and capital resources more efficiently. Through the use of online quizzes and labs, discussions and modules, tutorials and interactive content, the capital of online instruction can be used in place of traditional faculty labor. Through the use of undergraduate or graduate assistants, peer tutors, and faculty in a more targeted manner, lower-cost labor can be used in place of higher-cost labor. Through an expansion of online learning, capital investment in online courses can help institutions reduce the demand for on-campus classrooms and avoid or delay new capital construction.

The Holes

But we still have several holes in our understanding of the process whereby cost-efficiencies result from putting courses and educational programs online. As indicated, several parts of the framework proposed in the first chapter have not been researched well or at all, while other cells seem to have been addressed, although perhaps not comprehensively. Do not assume that research or understanding from an earlier era of distance education using technologies that are pre-Internet apply as well to online learning; they may or may not. We need research to see whether online learning is as different as some assert or just teaching and learning done online. We do not need more studies that compare courses—one offered in the traditional manner and the other online—that conclude "no significant difference" (see http://www.nosignificantdifference.org) and do not address questions about what specifically may be working well and what may not. To find the answers we need, researchers and institutions need to tackle portions of this research agenda over the next several years so that institutions can make better decisions and provide ever better education to online students.

The research may be quantitative or qualitative. We need multiple studies that use multiple methods to get a sense of the answer, and the repetition of studies in different institutions, contexts, and conditions can help build our understanding of how, when, and where cost-efficiencies are possible. In addition, many institutions need to conduct their own studies to make sure they are making wise decisions.

The remainder of this chapter is organized around the framework introduced in the first chapter and includes research questions for each element and factor.

The Elements

This section identifies "holes" in our understanding and is arranged by the framework outlined earlier. What research is needed that will answer remaining questions about the "elements?"

Crumbling Assumptions

It is intriguing to wonder whether some of the assumptions and wisdoms discussed earlier are still as commonly held. Is there evidence that the conventional wisdom is being eroded by those who lead or teach in higher education institutions? Is the assumption that cost and quality are permanently and closely related less prevalent in the minds of higher education leaders? Is the assumption that cost and enrollments are always correlated also less prevalent? Are there other signs that the conventional wisdom is under assault or revision? And while answers to these questions may not help us determine how to achieve cost-efficiencies, they will tell us whether more research is needed that directly examines the old assumptions about efficiency and quality.

Development

It is obvious that development costs are high but that development is necessary to reap any rewards through lower delivery costs. Although the research reviewed provides several examples of what to do to lower delivery costs, we do not know the extent to which an institution's learning curve can be improved. Can it help lower development costs? How much? How can development be done best (or most efficiently)?

We need more examples of low-cost or right-size online learning. Are there other small-scale applications similar to the small-scale chemistry examples? Can some learning still depend on low-cost applications, and what learning might require higher-cost applications?

More specifically, we know faculty are necessary to the development process, but we have less information about how faculty can achieve the benefits of development and design without an extensive design staff. To what extent can having faculty working alone (rather than with design teams) on course development lower these costs? What is lost and what is gained by doing so? This area of exploration is especially crucial, because not all courses can be slated for the higher-cost development of high-enrollment courses. The remainder of the courses will likely be developed by faculty, with cost-efficiencies achieved by faculty.

Delivery

The issues surrounding delivery costs are better understood. We know that it is the realm where higher development costs can translate into cost savings. But institutions still need to document the various delivery choices that lead to lower operating costs and give other institutions models to work from. How will moving to more constructivist learning models affect costs? Will standardizing course management systems across institutions or systems or states improve efficiency? What are the costs of standardization? Are there some delivery costs that cannot decline beyond a certain point?

Administration

We still need to document whether and how cost-efficiencies can result from the implementation of ERPs, portals, and online student services of all types. Institutions need to grapple with different models that allocate overhead costs to online courses. What are the breakeven points of different online programs? What choices led to different breakeven points? And are some costing methods better or more appropriate for online learning? If different costing methods lead to different results, what different insights do the methods lead to? And what are the results of costing? Are they strictly fiscal, or are there attitudinal changes as well? Has costing led to negative results?

The Factors

What research is needed to answer remaining questions about the "factors?"

Students

We know that students are crucial for achieving economies of scale. But we need a better understanding of the costs and cost benefits to students of online learning. How many and what kinds of students already have the requisite tools to learn online? Are these costs any different for students learning online but not on campus and those enrolled in regular classes but using online learning to augment coursework? In other words, are the costs to students for online learning any different from the costs of being a college student, by whatever means he or she is enrolled?

We know that online learning may not be the best choice for all students, but is it possible to help students who are not ready for online learning to become ready? How will having a large proportion of needy or passive students in an online course affect cost-efficiency? Are there ways to transform passive learners to active ones? For all students (not just the needy ones), what learning supports (peer tutors and technical aides, for example) are especially cost-effective for keeping students enrolled and successful? Will there come a time when learning supports are unnecessary? And why does online learning increase retention? What are the specific psychological reasons for it? When students drop out, is it because of something occurring in the online class or outside the institution's control? What is the cost of requiring student authentication in online learning courses? Is time an opportunity cost for only adult students or for all students? How much time do students put into learning online, and how does time matter to their learning if it is designed well? And is there any evidence that taking online courses helps students progress through their studies more efficiently or that institutions can enroll new students in spaces opened up for them by online students?

Faculty

Although we know a great deal about faculty and online learning, we still have some holes in our understanding. To what extent are young faculty different when it comes to online learning? Are they more efficient or capable? What tactics can help faculty handle the increased load of e-mails from all students or online discussions, and are they effective for student learning? How do faculty perceive their use of time when teaching online? We need more models that faculty can use to manage their time and student interactions.

The notion that the faculty job is changing is intriguing, although there is currently little evidence that it is happening in traditional institutions. Is the faculty role indeed being reshaped as Massy (2002) has suggested? Which faculty are being affected, how many are affected, where are they, and what disciplines are they in? What are the implications of these and subsequent changes to the profession for individuals and institutions? Is the faculty role being "unbundled"? Where? And if it is, what is the effect on individuals, institutions, and students? What evidence is there that unbundling results in better efficiency?

Are faculty as independent of institutional aims as McClure (1997) implies? Is this situation changing? Did the advent of online learning contribute to this change, or did other changes contribute to it? Are some faculty a barrier to online learning? What are their reasons, and are they legitimate? Can their concerns be addressed in some fashion?

When we turn to the issue of faculty's learning to teach online and to design more cost-efficient online courses, we need to know the most efficient ways to help faculty learn how to develop cost-efficient online courses. What is the learning curve for faculty? How do workload and family obligations affect the learning curve? Can it be documented, studied, and changed? Can the learning curve be changed, or is it a constant?

Other Staff

Two issues arose from the discussion of the growth in other staff on higher education campuses. How many of these new essential staff (essential for online learning) are there, and what costs do they add to an institution's budget? How do we assess the efficiency of the salaries of these staff, and are there ways to improve their efficiency?

Instructional Design

How much instructional design is necessary? Do we need large teams in all cases, or can it be streamlined in some fashion? What design steps or elements are absolutely essential, and what elements are nice to have if resources are available? Will there come a day when design is what faculty do?

We need more examples of substituting capital for labor, capital for capital, and lower-cost labor for higher-cost labor. People need to be able to see examples to be able to understand how the substitution can work well for student learning. We also need more examples of the capital-for-capital substitution that focus on using online learning to prevent or slow the growth of new buildings. What is saved by offering an online program? How many online courses make a building? How many new students can legitimately be served through online learning? And are students ready to learn in this fashion?

As for readiness, are some of the criteria more important than others? Are there effective ways to get ready? Will we need new criteria in the future, or will some of these criteria eventually be eliminated?

Must institutions and programs go through the levels of substitution noted by Twigg—moving from the add-on or bolt-on to the replacement model to the emporium model to the fully online model. Is this the standard or normal progression for each institution? Can the stages be leapfrogged? What are the advantages of proceeding through the stages? Or do different models help institutions match the appropriate technology (which may include face-to-face instruction or small-scale applications) with the appropriate student learning needs?

Content

This factor is largely unresearched. To what extent will using preexisting content affect development costs? How much time does it really take faculty to find, evaluate, and use learning objects? Is there a breakeven point for when it makes sense to invest in revising learning objects or an existing course? Can granularization of learning objects help faculty find and use learning objects more efficiently?

Will policies to encourage sharing content work? Are they necessary to make sharing happen? How well does repurposing instructional modules work? How much does it save? What are the short- and long-term effects of such sharing projects as the MIT OpenCourseWare project? Is MIT changing curricular design or content in degree programs offered by other higher education institutions?

What will be the impact of all of these sharing initiatives? Will OpenCourseWare have more or less an impact than learning objects?

Infrastructure

Some good answers about outsourcing and leasing have come out of the COSTS project, but we still need to learn to what extent outsourcing or leasing affects the cost-efficiency of online courses. And for those concerned about costing, what percentage of demand on the infrastructure do online courses account for? How should we rationalize the percentage of total infrastructure costs that online courses should cover?

Policies

Policy is the one area for which the least research and perhaps the greatest need exist. To what extent does offering a lower tuition rate (an in-state rate for out-of-state students, for example) or tuition waivers affect cost-efficiency or modify the breakeven point? To what extent does charging tuition at market value affect the viability of the program or access to the program for low-income students? To what extent does having a state subsidy affect cost-efficiency, and is it the brake on efficiency that some charge? What is the subsidy's effect on online learning? Are institutions charging a different rate for online students that includes paying for services they use more and excludes services they do not use? Does the practice of having one tuition rate for all courses—whether online or on campus—mean that the distinction among program types or delivery modes is eroding?

Although so much literature exists on policies that affect faculty, some may find it surprising that so many questions remain to be answered. Do policies on faculty workload help or hinder innovation? Does the choice of workload (in load or out of load) affect cost-efficiency or the breakeven point? Does a workload requirement (in terms of courses taught per term) affect involvement in online learning? Can differences in promotion and tenure policies increase faculty involvement in online learning? Do they have any relationship to cost-efficiency? What is the payoff of professional development for faculty? Is it strictly related to quality, or is there an impact on cost-efficiencies as well? Do different intellectual property policies affect innovation? Do policies that stress sharing the proceeds of intellectual property between the institution and faculty increase online learning, or do policies that return all proceeds to the institution decrease online learning? Do other policies regarding faculty work in addition to the practice of credit-based workload impede online learning?

It would be intriguing to know whether policies intended to shape student behavior work as expected. Do students respond to state or institutional policies that encourage them to use resources more efficiently? Do they respond more to rewards or to punishments? Do some of these policies work better than others? Do such policies have unintended consequences? What is the actual gain to institutions or states of the policies intended to shape student behavior? As more states and institutions consider such policies, solid policy research on existing efforts is needed.

Where are time policies strongest? Where does seat time still control academe? Can we document changes in the prevalence of class schedules, academic calendars, and office hours as online learning increases? Will open enrollment and self-paced learning increase, and why or why not?

Although it appears logical that planning helps one achieve a specific vision, we need a better understanding of how having a plan and vision affects online learning. Does having a vision or a strategic plan for online learning affect its success or cost-efficiency? If so, how and to what extent? Or do more influential forces (such as market forces, student demands, and the availability of technology) create change irrespective of having a strategic plan? What examples do we have of new "learning spaces," and how quickly are they being adopted? What evidence is there that such spaces actually encourage learning, and are they cost-effective?

To what extent does having a budget for an online program improve cost-efficiencies? Is its impact solely a fiscal one, or are there attitudinal changes involved as well? And as online learning increases and the number of redesigned courses challenge our perception of what a "good class size" is, will class sizes change? Will we find that assumptions about ideal or normal or negotiated class size change over time, or will online learning continue to follow the same rules as traditional courses?

Readers with additional questions are encouraged to take action to find answers and share them with colleagues.

The Research Challenge

Institutions offering online learning and attempting to maximize its cost-efficiency have a responsibility to help answer these questions. Getting answers will result from many smaller studies performed by different types of institutions working in multiple settings and with various media, disciplines, and organizations. It will likely be the sum of many smaller studies that provide insight into what ensures student learning and cost-efficiencies and what creates a level of comfort and confidence that both quality and efficiency can be achieved by going online.

Having unanswered questions about online learning, however, should not be used to forestall proceeding with further experiments and studies. Although room will always exist to develop better and more efficient online learning, enough answers or principles are available that the novice institution or faculty member can be assured that online learning is effective.

The larger challenge is not only achieving credibility for online learning but also understanding its advantages and disadvantages without devolving into partisan arguments that it is always or never better than current practices. Such arguments delay the time when research can provide the necessary guidance on how best to use it to achieve student learning while making the most efficient use of institutional resources and faculty time. Both ends can and must coexist. The challenges mentioned in the first chapter—growing numbers of students and constrained state resources—will not recede and in fact may play an even larger role in higher education's future. They will shape our responses to these and further challenges and subtly create new potential avenues by which our noblest aspirations can take form. Online learning can be such an avenue, as it makes higher education's aspiration to educate more people to ever higher levels of understanding a reality. It is an innovation that stirs the imagination and creativity of institutions and faculty and may well help us face the challenges with a flair for experimentation, a willingness to push the boundaries of our current knowledge, and a dedication to students and the institutions that make their learning a top priority.

References

Allen, I. E., and Seaman, J. (2004). Entering the mainstream. Needham, MA: Sloan Consortium. Retrieved June 6, 2005 from http://www.sloan-c.org/resources/entering_mainstream.pdf.

American Management Association. (2003a). And the cost-savings winner is . . . e-learning. *HR Focus, 80*(3), 4–6.

American Management Association. (2003b). The pay-offs of e-learning go far beyond the financial. *HR Focus, 80*(10), 7.

Arizona Learning Systems. (1998). Preliminary cost methodology for distance learning. Phoenix: State Board of Directors for Community Colleges.

Arnone, M. (2004a, January 8). State spending on colleges drops over all for first time in 11 years. *Chronicle of Higher Education.* Retrieved June 5, 2005 from http://chronicle.com/prm/daily/2004/01/2004010801n.htm.

Arnone, M. (2004b, February 6). Please leave, already. *Chronicle of Higher Education.* Retrieved Feb. 4, 2004 from http://chronicle.com/prm/weekly/v50/i22/22a02001.htm.

Arvan, L., and others. (1998). The SCALE efficiency projects. *Journal of Asynchronous Learning Networks, 2*(2), 33–60. Retrieved June 23, 2001 from http://www.aln.org/publications/jaln/v2n2/pdf/v2n2_arvan.pdf.

Ash, C. (2000). Towards a new cost-aware evaluation framework. *Educational Technology and Society, 3*(4). Retrieved Dec. 30, 2003 from http://ifets.ieee.org/periodical//vol_4_2000/ash.html.

Ash, C., and Bacsich, P. (1999). *Weighing air: Measuring the costs of learning technology in the UK.* Paper presented at the annual meeting of the Western Cooperative for Educational Telecommunications, November, Portland, OR.

Bacsich, P., and Ash, C. (1999). The hidden costs of networked learning: The impact of a costing framework on educational practice. Retrieved June 5, 2005 from http://www.shu.ac.uk/virtual_campus/cnl/papers/ascilite99.html.

Bartolic-Zlomislic, S., and Bates, A. W. (1999). Investing in online learning: Potential benefits and limitations. Retrieved Feb. 25, 2005 from http://bates.cstudies.ubc.ca/investing.html.

Bartolic-Zlomislic, S., and Brett, C. (1999). Assessing the costs and benefits of telelearning: A case study from the Ontario Institute for Studies in Education, University of Toronto. Retrieved Feb. 25, 2005 from http://research.cstudies.ubc.ca/nce/OISEcbreport.pdf.

Bates, A. W. (n.d.). Financial strategies and resources to support online learning. Retrieved Feb. 26, 2005 from http://eduspecs.ic.gc.ca/pub/e-learningresources/doc_financial_strategies/index.html.

Bates, A. W. (1995). *Technology, open learning and distance education.* London: Routledge.

Bates, A. W. (2000a). Distance education in dual mode higher education institutions: Challenges and changes. Retrieved Feb. 26, 2005 from http://bates.cstudies.ubc.ca/papers/challengesandchanges.html.

Bates, A. W. (2000b). *Managing technological change.* San Francisco: Jossey-Bass.

Betts, K. S. (1998). An institutional overview: Factors influencing faculty participation in distance education in postsecondary education in the United States. *Online Journal of Distance Learning Administration, 1*(3). Retrieved June 6, 2005 from http://www.westga.edu/~distance/betts13.html.

Bishop, T. (2002). Linking cost effectiveness with institutional goals: Best practices in online education. In Mayadas, F., Bourne, J., and Moore, J. C. (Eds.) *Elements of quality online education: Practice and direction* (pp. 75–86). Needham, MA: Sloan Consortium.

Bishop, T., and SchWeber, C. (2001). UMUC's online MBA program: A case study of cost-effectiveness and the implications for large-scale programs. In J. Bourne and J. C. Moore (Eds.), *Online education* (pp. 173–182). Needham, MA: Sloan Center for Online Education.

Bodain, Y., and Robert, J. (2000). Investigating distance learning on the Internet. Retrieved June 15, 2005 from http://www.isoc.org/inet2000/cdproceedings/6a/6a_4.htm.

Boettcher, J. V. (2004). *How much does it cost to develop a distance learning course? It all depends.* . . . Retrieved Feb. 11, 2005 from http://www.cren.net/~jboettch/dlmay.htm.

Breneman, D. W. (2002, June 14). For colleges, this is not just another recession. *Chronicle of Higher Education,* B7. Retrieved June 5, 2005 from http://chronicle.com/prm/weekly/v48/i40/40b00701.htm.

Brigham, D. (2003). Benchmark information survey. Unpublished presentation. Excelsior University: http://www.excelsioruniversity-edu.org/.

Brown, B. L. (1998). Applying constructivism in vocational and career education. ERIC Clearinghouse on Adult, Career, and Vocational Education. Retrieved Feb. 25, 2005 from http://ericacve.org/mp_brown_01.asp.

Brown, G., Myers, C. B., and Roy, S. (2003). Formal course design and the student learning experience. *Journal of Asynchronous Learning Networks, 7*(3), 66–76. Retrieved Dec. 10, 2003 from http://www.aln.org/publications/jaln/v7n3/v7n3_myers.asp.

Campbell, J. O., and others. (2004). Cost-effective distributed learning with electronics labs. *Journal of Asynchronous Learning Networks, 8*(3), 5–10. Retrieved Feb. 25, 2005 from http://www.sloan-c.org/publications/jaln/v8n3/pdf/v8n3_campbell.pdf.

Capper, J., and Fletcher, D. (1996). *Effectiveness and cost-effectiveness of print-based correspondence study.* Paper prepared for the Institute for Defense Analysis, Alexandria, VA.

Carnevale, D. (2005, June 28). Online courses continue to grow dramatically, enrolling nearly 1 million, report says. *Chronicle of Higher Education.* Retrieved June 31, 2005 from http://chronicle.com/daily/2005/06/20005062802t.htm.

Carr, S. (2001, February 16). Is anyone making money on distance education? *Chronicle of Higher Education, 47*(23), A41. Retrieved Sep 30, 2004 from http://chronicle.com/prm/weekly/v47/i23/23a04101.htm.

Chickering, A., and Ehrmann, S. C. (1996, October). Implementing the seven principles: Technology as lever. *AAHE Bulletin, 49*(1), 3–6. Retrieved June 30, 2002 from http://www.tltgroup.org/programs/seven.html.

Chickering, A. W., and Gamson, Z. F. (1987). Seven principles for good practice in undergraduate education. *AAHE Bulletin, 39*(7), 3–7. Retrieved June 30, 2002 from http://www.cord.edu/dept/assessment/sevenprin.htm.

Conference Board of Canada. (1991). *Employability skills profile: The critical skills required of the Canadian workforce.* Ottawa, ON: Conference Board of Canada.

Crawford, G., and Rudy, J. A. (2003). Top ten IT issues. *Educause Quarterly, 26*(2), 12–26. Retrieved Feb. 5, 2005 from http://www.educause.edu/ir/library/pdf/eqm0322.pdf.

Cukier, J. (1997). Cost-benefit analysis of telelearning: Development a methodology framework. *Distance Education, 18*(1), 137–152.

Daniel, J. (1996). *The multi-media mega-university: The hope for the 21st century.* Paper presented at the North of England Education Conference, January 2, 1997, Sheffield, England. Retrieved Nov. 23, 2004 from http://www.leeds.ac.uk/educol/documents/000000087.htm.

Daniel, J. (1997). *Mega-universities and knowledge media: Technology strategies for higher education.* London: Kogan Page.

Diaz, D. P. (2000, March/April). Carving a new path for distance education research. *Technology Source.* Retrieved Feb. 25, 2005 from http://horizon.unc.edu/TS/default.asp?show=articleandid=648.

Dolence, M. G., and Norris, D. M. (1995). *Transforming higher education: A vision for learning in the 21st century.* Ann Arbor, MI: Society for College and University Planning.

Drucker, P. F. (n.d.). The next information revolution. Retrieved Jan. 22, 2004 from http://www.versaggi.net/ecommerce/articles/drucker-inforevolt.htm.

Duderstadt, J. J. (1999). Can colleges and universities survive in the information age? In R. N. Katz and associates (Eds.), *Dancing with the devil* (pp. 1–26). San Francisco: Jossey-Bass.

DuMont, R. R. (2002). Distance learning: A systems view. Retrieved Feb. 25, 2005 from http://www.kent.edu/rcet/proposals/upload/DuMont-Final.doc.

Eggins, H. (2000). Costing technology-based education. In M. J. Finkelstein, C. Frances, F. I. Jewett, and B. W. Scholz (Eds.), *Dollars, distance, and online education* (pp. 63–81). Phoenix: Oryx Press.

Ehrmann, S. C. (1999). Asking the hard questions about technology use and education. *Change, 31*(2), 25–29.

Ehrmann, S. C. (2004). *Activity-based costing: Studying the shape of Jell-o.* Paper presented at the annual meeting of the Western Cooperative for Educational Telecommunications, November 11, San Antonio, TX.

Ellis, T., and Cohen, M. (2001). Integrating multimedia into a distance learning environment: Is the game worth the candle? *British Educational Communications and Technology, 32*(4), 495–497.

Fahy, P. J. (1998). Reflections on the productivity paradox and distance education technology. *Journal of Distance Education, 13*(2). Retrieved Jan. 9, 2004 from http://cade.athabascau.ca/vol13.2/fahy.html.

Feenberg, A. (1999). Distance learning: Promise or threat? Retrieved July 19, 1999 from http://www-rohan.sdsu.edu/faculty/feenberg/TELE3.HTM.

Finkelstein, M. J., and Scholz, B. W. (2000). Overview: What do we know about information technology and the cost of collegiate teaching and learning? In M. J. Finkelstein, C. Frances, F. I. Jewett, and B. W. Scholz (Eds.), *Dollars, distance, and online education* (pp. 3–34). Phoenix: Oryx Press.

Fisher, S., and Nygren, T. I. (2000). Experiments in the cost-effective uses of technology in teaching: Lessons from the Mellon program so far. Retrieved Feb. 25, 2005 from http://www.ceutt.org.

Foster, L. (2001). Technology: Transforming the landscape of higher education. *Review of Higher Education, 25*(1), 115–124.

Fredericksen, E., and others. (2000). Factors influencing faculty satisfaction with asynchronous teaching and learning in the SUNY learning network. *Journal of Asynchronous Learning Networks, 4*(3). Retrieved Feb. 25, 2005 from http://www.aln.org/alnweb/journal/Vol4_issue3/fs/Fredericksen/fs-fredericksen.htm.

Friedman, T. L. (2005). *The world is flat.* New York: Farrar, Straus & Giroux.

Frydenberg, J. (2002). Quality standards in eLearning: A matrix of analysis. *International Review of Research in Open and Distance Learning, 3*(2). Retrieved June 16, 2005 from http://www.irrodl.org/content/v3.2/frydenberg.html.

Geith, C. (2003). The costs of learner-centered online learning: An exploratory case study. In F. Mayadas, J. Bourne, and J. C. Moore (Eds.), *Elements of Quality Online Education: Practice and Direction* (Vol. 4, pp. 87–101). Needham, MA: Sloan Consortium.

Geith, C., and Cometa, M. (1999). Cost analysis results: Comparing distance learning and on-campus courses. Retrieved May 10, 2006 from http://www.rit.edu/~609www/ch/faculty/CostStudy.PDF.pdf.

Geith, C., and Vignare, K. (2001). Online degree programs: Service and cost. In J. Bourne and J. C. Moore (Eds.), *Online education* (pp. 203–211). Needham, MA: Sloan Center for Online Education.

Goldberg, E. D., and Seldin, D. M. (2000). The future of higher education in an Internet world. In M. J. Finkelstein, C. Frances, F. I. Jewett, and B. W. Scholz (Eds.), *Dollars, distance, and online education* (pp. 296–313). Phoenix: Oryx Press.

Graves, W. H. (1994). Toward a national learning infrastructure. *Educom Review, 29*(2). Retrieved June 15, 2005 from http://www.educause.edu/pub/er/review/ reviewArticles/29232.html.

Green, K. C. (1997). Think twice—and businesslike—about distance education. *AAHE Bulletin, 50*(2), 3–6.

Green, K. C. (1998). 1998 National survey of information technology in higher education. Encino, CA: Campus Computing Project. Retrieved June 15, 2005 from http://www.campuscomputing.net.

Green, K. C. (2000). What is information technology in higher education? In M. J. Finkelstein, C. Frances, F. I. Jewett, and B. W. Scholz (Eds.), *Dollars, distance, and online education* (pp. 48–62). Phoenix: Oryx Press.

Green, K. C. (2002a). Campus portals make progress; technology budgets suffer significant cuts. Retrieved Feb. 25, 2005 from http://www.campuscomputing.net/summaries/ 2002/index.html.

Green, K. C. (2002b). Coming of age in academe. *Converge Magazine.* Retrieved Feb. 4, 2004 from http://www.convergemag.com/magazine/story.phtml?id=29718.

Green, K., and Jenkins, R. (1998, March). IT financial planning 101. *NACUBO Business Officer,* 32–37.

Hagner, P. R., and Schneebeck, C. A. (2001). Engaging the faculty. In C. A. Barone and P. R. Hagner (Eds.), *Technology-mediated teaching and learning* (pp. 1–12). San Francisco: Jossey-Bass. Retrieved May 10, 2006 from http://media.wiley.com/product_data/excerpt/ 30/07879501/0787950130.pdf.

Harkness, W. L., Lane, J. L., and Harwood, J. T. (2003). A cost-effective model for teaching elementary statistics with improved student performance. *Journal of Asynchronous Learning Networks, 7*(2), 8–17. Retrieved June 2, 2005 from http://www.aln.org/ publications/jaln/v7n2/pdf/v7n2_harkness.pdf.

Harley, D., Maher, M., Henke, J., and Lawrence, S. (2003). An analysis of technology enhancements in a large lecture course. *Educause Quarterly, 26*(3), 26–33. Retrieved June 15, 2005 from http://www.educause.edu/ir/library/pdf/eqm0335.pdf.

Hartman, J., Dziuban, C., and Moskal, P. (2000). Faculty satisfaction in ALNs: A dependent or independent variable? *Journal of Asynchronous Learning Networks, 4*(3), 155–179. Retrieved Feb. 15, 2005 from http://www.aln.org/publications/jaln/v4n3/pdf/v4n3_ hartman.pdf.

Henderson, T. (2004). *Using activity-based costing to inform university assessment.* Paper presented at the annual meeting of the Western Cooperative for Educational Telecommunications, November 11, San Antonio, TX.

Heterick, R. C. (1995). Confronting the four horsemen. Retrieved June 15, 2005 from http://www.educause.edu/nlii/meetings/orleans95/horsemen.html.

Hislop, G. W. (2001a). *Does teaching online take more time?* Paper presented at the 31st ASEE/IEEE Frontiers in Education Conference, October 10–13, Reno, NV. Retrieved Feb. 15, 2005 from http://fie.engrng.pitt.edu/fie2001/papers/ 1198.pdf.

Hislop, G. W. (2001b). Operating cost of an online degree program. In J. Bourne and J. C. Moore (Eds.), *Online education* (pp. 189–202). Needham, MA: Sloan Center for Online Education.

Howell, S. L., Williams, P. B., and Lindsay, N. K. (2003). Thirty-two trends affecting distance education: An informed foundation for strategic planning. *Online Journal of Distance Education, 6*(3). Retrieved Dec. 12, 2003 from http://www.westga.edu/~distance/ojdla/fall63/howell63.html.

Jewett, F. (2000). Case studies in evaluating the benefits and costs of mediated instruction/distributed learning. Retrieved June 15, 2005 from http://www.calstate.edu/special_projects.

Jewett, F., and Henderson, T. (2003). The technology costing methodology project: Collecting and interpreting instructional cost data. *Planning for Higher Education, 32*(1), 15–27.

Johnstone, S. M. (2002). Signs of the times: Change is coming for e-learning. *Educause Review, 37*(6), 15–24. Retrieved Feb. 10, 2005 from http://www.educause.edu/ir/library/pdf/erm0260.pdf.

Jones, D. (2001). *Technology costing methodology handbook, Version 1.0.* Boulder, CO: Western Cooperative for Educational Telecommunications. Retrieved Feb. 15, 2005 from http://www.wcet.info/projects/tcm/TCM_Handbook_Final.pdf.

Jones, D., and Matthews, D. (2002). The transformation of instruction by information technology: Implications for state higher education policy. Retrieved Feb. 10, 2005 from http://www.wcet.info/projects/tcm/files/whitepaper1.pdf.

Jung, I., and Rha, I. (2000). Effectiveness and cost-effectiveness of online education: A review of the literature. *Educational Technology, 40*(4), 57–60.

Katz, R. N., and Rudy, J. A. (Eds.) (1999). *Information technology in higher education: Assessing its impact and planning for the future.* San Francisco: Jossey-Bass.

Keehn, A. K., and Norris, D. M. (2003, November 1). IT planning: Cultivating innovation and value. *Syllabus Magazine.* Retrieved Dec. 30, 2003 from http://www.syllabus.com/article.asp?id=8454.

King, J. W., and others. (2002). Policy frameworks for distance education: Implications for decision makers. *Online Journal of Distance Learning Administration, 3*(2). Retrieved Dec. 30, 2003 from http://www.westga.edu/~distance.king32.html.

Landry, S. G. (2000). Costs of ubiquitous computing. In M. J. Finkelstein, C. Frances, F. I. Jewett, and B. W. Scholz (Eds.), *Dollars, distance, and online education* (pp. 199–212). Phoenix: Oryx Press.

Lasseter, M., and Rogers, M. (2004). Creating flexible e-learning through the use of learning objects. *Educause Quarterly, 27*(4). Retrieved Feb. 10, 2005 from http://www.educause.edu/ir/library/pdf/eqm04410.pdf.

Leach, K., and Smallen, D. (1998). What do information technology support services really cost? *CAUSE/EFFECT, 21*(2), 38–45. Retrieved Dec. 27, 2003 from http://www.educause.edu/ir/library/html/cnc9856/cnc9856.html.

Leach, K., and Smallen, D. (2000). Understanding the COSTS of information technology (IT) support services in higher education. In M. J. Finkelstein, C. Frances, F. I. Jewett, and B. W. Scholz (Eds.), *Dollars, distance, and online education* (pp. 123–139). Phoenix: Oryx Press.

Levin, H. (1983). *Cost-effectiveness: A primer.* Beverly Hills, CA: Sage.

Levin, H. M., and McEwan, P. J. (2001). *Cost-effectiveness analysis* (2nd ed.). Thousand Oaks, CA: Sage.

Littlejohn, A. (Ed.). (2003). *Reusing online resources: A sustainable approach to e-learning.* London: Kogan Page.

Lockee, B., Moore, M., and Burton, J. (2002). Measuring success: Evaluation strategies for distance education. *Educause Quarterly, 25*(1), 20–26. Retrieved Feb. 10, 2005 from http://www.educause.edu/ir/library/pdf/eqm0213.pdf.

Looney, M. A., and Sheehan, M. (2001). Digitizing education: A primer on eBooks. *Educause Review, 36*(4), 38–46. Retrieved Feb. 15, 2005 from http://www.educause.edu/ir/library/pdf/erm0142.pdf.

Maltz, L., DeBlois, P. B., and the Educause Current Issues Committee. (2005). Top ten IT issues, 2005. *Educause Review, 40*(3), 15–28. Retrieved June 15, 2005 from http://www.educause.edu/ir/library/pdf/erm0530.pdf.

Mason, R., Pegler, C., and Weller, M. (2005). A learning object success story. *Journal of Asynchronous Learning Networks, 9*(1), 97–105. Retrieved June 15, 2005 from http://www.sloan-c.org/publications/jaln/v9n1/pdf/v9n1_mason.pdf.

Massachusetts Institute of Technology. (2005). *2004 program evaluation findings report.* Retrieved Jan. 15, 2006 from http://ocw.mit.edu/NR/rdonlyres/90C9BC91–7819–48A0–9E9A-D6B2701C1CE5/0/MIT_OCW_2004_ Program_Eval.pdf.

Massy, W. F. (2002). *Life on the wired campus: How information technology will shape institutional futures.* Stanford, CA: National Center for Postsecondary Improvement, Stanford University. Retrieved Dec. 23, 2003 from http://www.stanford.edu/group/ncpi/documents/pdfs/6–02_wiredcampus.pdf.

Massy, W. F. (2003). *Honoring the trust: Quality and cost containment in higher education.* New York: Anker Publishing.

Massy, W. F., and Zemsky, R. (1995) Using information technology to enhance academic productivity. Retrieved Feb. 10, 2005 from http://www.educause.edu/nlii/keydocs/massy.html.

McClure, P. A. (1997). What will "transformation" mean to traditional universities? *Virginia.edu, 1*(2). Retrieved Dec. 30, 2003 from http://www.itc.Virginia.edu/Virginia.edu/fall97/trans/all.html.

McCollum, K. (1999, February 19). Colleges struggle to manage technology's rising costs. *Chronicle of Higher Education, 45*(24), A27. Retrieved Feb. 16, 1999 from http://www.chronicle.com/free/v45/i24/24a00101.htm.

Meyer, K. A. (2002a). Does policy make a difference? An exploration into policies for distance education. *Online Journal of Distance Learning Administration, 5*(4). Retrieved Feb. 10, 2005 from http://www.westga.edu/~distance/ojdla/winter54/Meyer_policy_54.htm.

Meyer, K. A. (2002b). *Quality in distance education: Focus on on-line learning.* ASHE-ERIC Higher Education Report, Vol. 29, No. 4. San Francisco: Jossey-Bass. (ED 470 042)

Meyer, K. A. (2003). The rule of the marketplace: How flawed beliefs contributed to the failure of dot-coms and other new virtual U[niversitie]s. *Educause Quarterly, 26*(2), 4–7. Retrieved June 10, 2005 from http://www.educause.edu/ir/library/pdf/eqm0320.pdf.

Meyer, K. A. (2005). Planning for cost-efficiencies in online learning. *Planning for Higher Education, 33*(3), 19–30.

Meyer, K. A. (forthcoming). Method (and madness) of assessing online discussions. Accepted for publication in *Journal of Asynchronous Learning Networks*.

Milam, J. (2000). *Cost analysis of online courses.* Paper presented at an annual forum of the Association for Institutional Research, May 21–23, Cincinnati, OH.

Miller, G. E. (2001). Penn State's World Campus: A case study in achieving cost efficiencies in ALN. In J. Bourne and J. C. Moore (Eds.), *Online education* (pp. 163–172). Needham, MA: Sloan Center for Online Education.

Montgomery, C. H., and King, D. W. (2002). Comparing library and user related costs of print and electronic journal collections. *D-Lib Magazine, 8,* 10. Retrieved October 23, 2002 from http://www.dlib.org/dlib/october02/Montgomery/10montgomery.html.

Moonen, J. (1997). The efficiency of telelearning. *Journal of Asynchronous Learning Networks, 1*(2). Retrieved Dec. 30, 2003 from http://www.aln.org/publications/jaln/v1n2/v1n2_moonen.asp.

Morgan, B. M. (2000). Is distance learning worth it? Helping to determine the costs of online courses. Retrieved Dec. 30, 2003 from http://www.marshall.edu/distance/distancelearning.pdf.

National Association of College and University Business Officers. (2002). *Explaining college costs.* Retrieved June 15, 2005 from http://www.nacubo.org/documents/research/cofcfinalreport.pdf.

National Center for Education Statistics. (1996). *Fall staff in postsecondary institutions, 1993* (NCES 1996–323). Washington, DC: U.S. Department of Education.

National Center for Education Statistics. (1998). *Fall staff in postsecondary institutions, 1995* (NCES 1998–228). Washington, DC: U.S. Department of Education.

National Center for Education Statistics. (1999). *Distance education at postsecondary education institutions: 1997–98.* Retrieved Dec. 23, 2003 from http://nces.ed.gov/pubsearch/pubsinfo.asp?pubid_00013.

National Center for Education Statistics. (2000a). *Distance education at postsecondary institutions: 1997–98* (NCES 2000–013). Washington, DC: U.S. Department of Education.

National Center for Education Statistics. (2000b). *Fall staff in postsecondary institutions, 1997* (NCES 2000–164). Washington, DC: U.S. Department of Education.

National Center for Education Statistics. (2002a). *Distance education instruction by postsecondary faculty and staff: Fall 1998* (NCES 2002–155). Washington, DC: U.S. Department of Education.

National Center for Education Statistics. (2002b). *Projections of education statistics to 2012* (NCES 2002–030). Washington, DC: U.S. Department of Education.

National Center for Education Statistics. (2003). *Distance education at degree-granting postsecondary institutions: 2000–2001* (NCES 2003–017). Washington, DC: U.S. Department of Education.

National Commission on the Cost of Higher Education. (1998). *Straight talk about college costs and prices.* Retrieved June 10, 2005 from http://www.nyu.edu/classes/jepsen/costreport.html.

National Education Association. (2000). *Quality on the line.* Washington, DC: Institute for Higher Education Policy.

National Small-Scale Chemistry Center. (n.d.). Laboratory content, consumables, and experiment specific equipment cost correlations. Retrieved Feb. 25, 2006 from http://www.smallscalechemistry.colostate.edu/cost_correlation.html.

Noone, L. P., and Swenson, C. (2001). Five dirty little secrets in higher education. *Educause Review, 36*(6), 20–31. Retrieved Feb. 10, 2005 from http://www.educause.edu/ir/library/pdf/erm0161.pdf.

Nygren, T. I., and Fisher, S. (1999). Cost-effective uses of technology in teaching: Current issues and future prospects. Retrieved Dec. 30, 2003 from http://www.ceutt.org/CEUTTx98.htm.

Oblinger, D. (1999). Putting students at the center: A planning guide to distributed learning. Boulder, CO: Educause. Retrieved Feb. 10, 2005 from http://www.educause.edu/LibraryDetailPage/666?ID=PUB3401.

Prensky, M. (2001). Digital natives, digital immigrants. *On the Horizon, 9*(5), 1–6. Retrieved June 10, 2005 from http://www.marcprensky.com/writing/Prensky%20-%20Digital%20Natives,%20Digital%20Immigrants%20-%20Part1.pdf.

Pumerantz, R., and Frances, C. (2000). Wide-angle view of the costs of introducing new technologies to the instructional program. In M. J. Finkelstein, C. Frances, F. I. Jewett, and B. W. Scholz (Eds.), *Dollars, distance, and online education* (pp. 241–255). Phoenix: Oryx Press.

Robinson, E. T. (2001). Maximizing the return on investment for distance education offerings. *Online Journal of Distance Learning Administration, 4*(3). Retrieved Dec. 30, 2003 from http://www.westga.edu/~distance/ojdla/fall43/robinson43.html.

Rockwell, S. K., Schauer, J., Fritz, S., and Marx, D. B. (1999). Incentives and obstacles influencing higher education faculty and administrators to teach via distance. *Online Journal of Distance Learning Administration, 2*(4). Retrieved Dec. 30, 2003 from http://www.westga.edu/~distance/rockwell24.html.

Rogers, E. M. (1995). *Diffusion of innovations.* New York: Free Press.

Rumble, G. (n.d.). The costs of networked learning: What have we learnt? Retrieved June 2, 2005 from http://www.shu.ac.uk/flish/rumblep.htm.

Rumble, G. (1997). *The costs and economics of open and distance learning.* London: Kogan Page.

Rumble, G. (2001). The costs and costing of networked learning. *Journal of Asynchronous Learning Networks, 5*(2), 75–96. Retrieved Dec. 23, 2003 from http://www.aln.org/publications/jaln/v5n2/pdf/v5n2_rumble.pdf.

Schifter, C. (2000). Faculty influencing faculty participation in distance education: A faculty analysis. *ED at a Distance, 13*(1). Retrieved Jan. 10, 2001 from http://www.usdla.org/ED_magazine/illuminactive/JAN00_Issue/Factors.htm.

Schifter, C. (2002). Perception differences about participating in distance education. *Online Journal of Distance Learning Administration, 5*(1). Retrieved Dec. 23, 2003 from http://www.westga.edu/~distance/ojdla/spring51/schifter51.html.

Senge, P. (1990). *The fifth discipline.* New York: Doubleday.

Smart, K., and Meyer, K. A. (2005). Changing course management systems: Lessons learned while converting a Blackboard course to Desire2Learn. *Educause Quarterly, 28*(2), 68–70. Retrieved Feb. 10, 2006 from http://www.educause.edu/ir/library/pdf/eqm05210.pdf.

Smith, B. (2000). Academia online: Education trends. *Elearning!* Retrieved Dec. 15, 2002 fromhttp://www.elearningmag.com/issues/may00/academia.htm.

Swan, K. (2003). Learning effectiveness: What the research tells us. In F. Mayadas, J. Bourne, and J. C. Moore (Eds.), *Elements of quality online education: Practice and direction* (Vol. 4, pp. 13–45). Needham, MA: Sloan Consortium.

Twigg, C. A. (1999). Improving learning and reducing costs: Redesigning large enrollment courses. Troy, NY: Center for Academic Transformation at Rensselaer Polytechnic Institute.

Twigg, C. A. (2002). Improving learning and reducing costs: Lessons learned from round I of the Pew Grant Program in Course Redesign. Retrieved Dec. 23, 2003 from http://center.rpi.edu/PewGrant/Rd1intro.html.

Twigg, C. A. (2003a). Improving quality and reducing cost: Designs for effective learning. *Change, 35*(4), 23–29.

Twigg, C. A. (2003b). Improving quality and reducing costs: New models for online learning. *Educause Review, 38*(5), 28–38. Retrieved Feb. 10, 2005 from http://www.educause.edu/ir/library/pdf/erm0352.pdf.

Twigg, C. A. (2005). Improving quality and reducing costs: The case for redesign. In *Course corrections* (pp. 32–49). Retrieved Feb. 10, 2006 from http://www.collegecost.info/pdfs/solution_papers/Collegecosts_Oct2005.pdf.

University of Delaware. (2002). Descriptive summary: National study of instructional costs and productivity. Retrieved Feb. 10, 2006 from http://www.udel.edu/IR/cost/brochure.html.

VanSlyke, T. (2003, May/June). Digital natives, digital immigrants: Some thoughts from the generation gap. *On the Horizon,* 2003. Retrieved May 2, 2003 from http://tsmivu.org/default.asp?show=articleandid=1011.

Waddoups, G. L., Hatch, G. L., and Butterworth, S. (2003). Balancing efficiency and effectiveness in first year reading and writing. In F. Mayadas, J. Bourne, and J. C. Moore (Eds.), *Elements of quality online education: Practice and direction* (Vol. 4, pp. 103–115). Needham, MA: Sloan Consortium.

Weinstein, L. (1993). *Moving a battleship with your bare hands.* Madison, WI: Magna Publications.

Wentling, T. L., and Park, J. (2001). Cost efficiency of online instruction in a research one university: A case study of a department's effort. In J. Bourne and J. C. Moore (Eds.), *Online education* (pp. 149–161). Needham, MA: Sloan Center for Online Education.

Wentling, T. L., and Park, J. (2002). Cost analysis of e-learning: A case study of a university program. Retrieved Feb. 15, 2005 from http://learning.ncsa.uiuc.edu/papers/ AHRD2002_Wentling-Park.pdf.

Whalen, T., and Wright, D. (1999). Methodology for cost-benefit analysis of web-based tele-learning: Case study of the Bell online institute. *The American Journal of Distance Education, 13*(1), 25, 43. Retrieved May 8, 2006 from http://www.uni-oldenburg. de/zef/cde/ econ/readings/whalen99.pdf.

White, L. (2003). Deconstructing the public-private dichotomy in higher education. *Change, 35*(3), 48–54.

Name Index

S

Schauer, J., 77
Schifter, C., 77
Schneebeck, C. A., 78
Scholz, B. W., 3, 5, 17, 40–42, 47, 48, 53, 86
SchWeber, C., 9, 33
Seaman, J., 5
Seldin, D. M., 78, 79, 85
Senge, P., 83
Sheehan, M., 67
Smallen, D., x, 9, 31, 71, 72
Smart, K., 32
Smith, B., 75
Swan, K., 5
Swenson, C., 82

T

Twigg, C. A., 38, 40, 54–57, 60–64, 89,
    92, 101

V

VanSlyke, T., 40
Vignare, K., 23, 45

W

Waddoups, G. L., 55, 56, 84
Weinstein, L., 91
Weller, M., 68
Wentling, T. L., 33, 74,
    86, 87
Whalen, T., 24
White, L., 1
Williams, P. B., 67
Wright, D., 24

Z

Zemsky, R., 5, 27, 50

Subject Index

A
Activity-based Costing method (ABC), 9, 10, 34
Administration, online learning, vii
   cost of, 28–34
   element, 19–20
   questions, 98
American Chemical Society, 61
American Management Association, 41, 48
Anadolu University (Turkey), 4
Arizona Learning Systems, 24, 41
Assumptions, crumbling, 97

B
Baruch College, 62
Blackboard, 30
Breakeven point, viii, 17
Brigham Young University, 55
Budgeting, viii, 86
Buffet Model, 64

C
California State University system, 27, 66, 80
Canada, 24, 32
Canadian universities, 2
   telelearning projects, 32
Capital
   versus labor, 55–58
   substituting capital for, 58
Carnegie Mellon University, 61
Class size, 86–87

CMS. *See* Course management system (CMS)
Conference Board of Canada, 2
Content factor, 64–69, 101–102
Cost
   of classroom instruction, 17 *Fig. 3*
   conventional wisdom on, 12
   of costing, 34
   of development, 20–25
   of mediated/online instruction, 16 *Fig. 2*
   methodologies, viii
   for various types of instruction, 18 *Fig. 4*
Cost of Supporting Technology Services (COSTS), 9, 31, 71, 102
Cost-benefit, definition of, 8
Cost-efficiencies
   definition of, 7, 8
   framework for unraveling research on, 6–7
   necessary assumptions about, 11–13
   reason for interest in, 1–6
   tools, 7–11
Costs,
   fixed, viii, 15, 16
   variable, viii, 15, 16
Course management system (CMS), 19–20, 32, 52
Course readiness criteria, 63
Credit-hours (SCHs), 34
Crossover point, 17

Median family income, 2
Medicare, 2
Mega-universities, 4
Mellon Foundation, 54
MERLOT. *See* Multimedia Educational Resources for Learning and Online Teaching
Michigan State University, 61
Minnesota, 32
MIT. *See* Massachusetts Institute of Technology
Morgan online costing tool, 9
Multimedia Educational Resources for Learning and Online Teaching (MERLOT), 66

N

NACUBO. *See* National Association of College and University Business Officers
National Association of College and University Business Officers (NACUBO), 9
National Center for Academic Transformation, 54
National Center for Education Statistics, 2, 5, 35, 43, 44, 50, 52, 69, 70, 74
National Commission on the Cost of Higher Education, 2
National Education Association (NEA), 43, 44, 50, 76
National Small-Scale Chemistry Center, 54
NEA. *See* National Education Association
No Child Left Behind, 4
North Dakota, 32

O

Online instruction, cost of, 16 *Fig. 2*
Online learning, 4, 5, 12
    and discussion forums, 60
    research on elements of, 15–36
    terms in, 15–19
Open University, 4, 17, 19, 48, 67, 80
OpenCourseWare (MIT), 65–67
Outputs, viii, 8

P

Payame Noor University (Iran), 4
Pennsylvania State University, 37, 48, 55, 56, 61, 62
Pew Charitable Trusts, 54
Policies, 73–87, 102–103
    budgeting, 83–886
    class size, 86–87
    and institute's vision, 83–84
    and sharing content, 81
    and strategic planning process, 84–86
    students, 80–81
    time issues in, 81–83
    on tuition and fees, 73–75
Portland State University, 56
Productivities, definition of, 8
Program in Course Redesign (National Center for Academic Transformation), 54
Program in Course Redesign (Twigg), 38

Q

Quality, viii, 5
    conventional wisdom on, 12
Quality in Distance Education: Focus on On-Line Learning (ASHE-ERIC Higher Education Report), vii, xiii, 5

R

Readiness criteria, 89
Reengineering, 57
Replacement Model, 63–64
Research challenge, 104
Rio Salado College, 58–59, 62, 64
Riverside Community College, 37
Rochester Institute of Technology, 23

S

Scalability, 27
Scale, economies of, 27, 95
Scope creep, 57
Seton Hall University, 72
Seven principles, 59–61
Sloan Foundation, 54
Spain, 65–66
Staff factor, 51–54, 100

About the Author

Katrina A. Meyer is associate professor of higher and adult education at the University of Memphis. She was previously an assistant professor of educational leadership at the University of North Dakota, where she authored the ASHE-ERIC Higher Education Report *Quality in Distance Education: Focus on On-Line Learning* (2002). She was director of distance learning and technology for the University and Community College System of Nevada and a member of the Nevada Commission on Educational Technology. Prior to this, she served eight years as associate director of academic affairs for the Higher Education Coordinating Board in the state of Washington and was responsible for technology planning and online learning issues. During this time, she wrote *Faculty Workload Studies: Perspectives, Needs, and Future Directions* (1998) for the ASHE-ERIC Higher Education Report series.

Dr. Meyer has been chair and vice chair of the Steering Committee for the Western Cooperative for Educational Telecommunications and an active participant since 1991. Most recently, she completed evaluations of two online learning projects for the Fund for the Improvement of Postsecondary Education.

About the ASHE Higher Education Report Series

Since 1983, the ASHE (formerly ASHE-ERIC) Higher Education Report Series has been providing researchers, scholars, and practitioners with timely and substantive information on the critical issues facing higher education. Each monograph presents a definitive analysis of a higher education problem or issue, based on a thorough synthesis of significant literature and institutional experiences. Topics range from planning to diversity and multiculturalism, to performance indicators, to curricular innovations. The mission of the Series is to link the best of higher education research and practice to inform decision making and policy. The reports connect conventional wisdom with research and are designed to help busy individuals keep up with the higher education literature. Authors are scholars and practitioners in the academic community. Each report includes an executive summary, review of the pertinent literature, descriptions of effective educational practices, and a summary of key issues to keep in mind to improve educational policies and practice.

The Series is one of the most peer reviewed in higher education. A National Advisory Board made up of ASHE members reviews proposals. A National Review Board of ASHE scholars and practitioners reviews completed manuscripts. Six monographs are published each year and they are approximately 120 pages in length. The reports are widely disseminated through Jossey-Bass and John Wiley & Sons, and they are available online to subscribing institutions through Wiley InterScience (http://www.interscience.wiley.com).

Call for Proposals

The ASHE Higher Education Report Series is actively looking for proposals. We encourage you to contact one of the editors, Dr. Kelly Ward (kaward@wsu.edu) or Dr. Lisa Wolf-Wendel (lwolf@ku.edu), with your ideas.

Recent Titles

Back Issue/Subscription Order Form

Copy or detach and send to:
Jossey-Bass, A Wiley Imprint, 989 Market Street, San Francisco CA 94103-1741

Call or fax toll-free: Phone 888-378-2537 6:30AM – 3PM PST; Fax 888-481-2665

Back Issues: Please send me the following issues at $26 each
(Important: please include series abbreviation and issue number.
For example AEHE 28:1)

_____

_____

_____

$ _____   Total for single issues

$ _____   SHIPPING CHARGES: SURFACE   Domestic Canadian

		First Item	$5.00	$6.00
		Each Add'l Item	$3.00	$1.50

For next-day and second-day delivery rates, call the number listed above.

Subscriptions   Please ❏ start ❏ renew my subscription to *ASHE Higher Education Reports* for the year 2_____ at the following rate:

U.S.	❏ Individual $165	❏ Institutional $185
Canada	❏ Individual $165	❏ Institutional $245
All Others	❏ Individual $201	❏ Institutional $296
	❏ Online subscriptions available too!	

**For more information about online subscriptions, visit
www.interscience.wiley.com**

$ _____   Total single issues and subscriptions (Add appropriate sales tax for your state for single issue orders. No sales tax for U.S. subscriptions. Canadian residents, add GST for subscriptions and single issues.)

❏Payment enclosed (U.S. check or money order only)
❏VISA ❏ MC ❏ AmEx ❏ #_____ Exp. Date _____

Signature _____ Day Phone _____
❏ Bill Me (U.S. institutional orders only. Purchase order required.)

Purchase order # _____
     Federal Tax ID13559302   GST 89102 8052

Name _____

Address _____

_____

Phone _____ E-mail _____

For more information about Jossey-Bass, visit our Web site at www.josseybass.com

ASHE-ERIC HIGHER EDUCATION REPORT IS NOW AVAILABLE ONLINE AT WILEY INTERSCIENCE

What is Wiley InterScience?

Wiley InterScience is the dynamic online content service from John Wiley & Sons delivering the full text of over 300 leading scientific, technical, medical, and professional journals, plus major reference works, the acclaimed Current Protocols laboratory manuals, and even the full text of select Wiley print books online.

What are some special features of Wiley InterScience?

Wiley Interscience Alerts is a service that delivers table of contents via e-mail for any journal available on Wiley InterScience as soon as a new issue is published online.
Early View is Wiley's exclusive service presenting individual articles online as soon as they are ready, even before the release of the compiled print issue. These articles are complete, peer-reviewed, and citable.
CrossRef is the innovative multi-publisher reference linking system enabling readers to move seamlessly from a reference in a journal article to the cited publication, typically located on a different server and published by a different publisher.

How can I access Wiley InterScience?

Visit http://www.interscience.wiley.com.

Guest Users can browse Wiley InterScience for unrestricted access to journal Tables of Contents and Article Abstracts, or use the powerful search engine.
Registered Users are provided with a *Personal Home Page* to store and manage customized alerts, searches, and links to favorite journals and articles. Additionally, Registered Users can view free Online Sample Issues and preview selected material from major reference works.
Licensed Customers are entitled to access full-text journal articles in PDF, with select journals also offering full-text HTML.

How do I become an Authorized User?

Authorized Users are individuals authorized by a paying Customer to have access to the journals in Wiley InterScience. For example, a University that subscribes to Wiley journals is considered to be the Customer.
Faculty, staff and students authorized by the University to have access to those journals in Wiley InterScience are Authorized Users. Users should contact their Library for information on which Wiley journals they have access to in Wiley InterScience.

ASK YOUR INSTITUTION ABOUT WILEY INTERSCIENCE TODAY!